MARTIN R. DELANY

SELECTED WRITINGS

MARTIN R. DELANY

SELECTED WRITINGS

a *Broadview Anthology of American Literature* edition

General Editors, *The Broadview Anthology of American Literature*:

Derrick R. Spires, Cornell University
Rachel Greenwald Smith, Saint Louis University
Christina Roberts, Seattle University
Joseph Rezek, Boston University
Justine S. Murison, University of Illinois, Urbana-Champaign
Laura L. Mielke, University of Kansas
Christopher Looby, University of California, Los Angeles
Rodrigo Lazo, University of California, Irvine
Alisha Knight, Washington College
Hsuan L. Hsu, University of California, Davis
Michael Everton, Simon Fraser University
Christine Bold, University of Guelph

broadview press

BROADVIEW PRESS – www.broadviewpress.com
Peterborough, Ontario, Canada

Founded in 1985, Broadview Press remains a wholly independent publishing house. Broadview's focus is on academic publishing: our titles are accessible to university and college students as well as scholars and general readers. With over 800 titles in print, Broadview has become a leading international publisher in the humanities, with world-wide distribution. Broadview is committed to environmentally responsible publishing and fair business practices.

Library and Archives Canada Cataloguing in Publication

Title: Martin R. Delany : selected writings.
Other titles: Works. Selections
Names: Delany, Martin Robison, 1812-1885, author. | Delany, Martin Robison, 1812-1885. Blake. Selections.
Description: Broadview anthology of American literature edition. | Series statement: The Broadview anthology of American literature | Includes bibliographical references.
Identifiers: Canadiana (print) 20230135390 | Canadiana (ebook) 20230158331 | ISBN 9781554816330 (softcover) | ISBN 9781770488946 (PDF) | ISBN 9781460408261 (EPUB)
Classification: LCC PS1534.D134 A6 2023 | DDC 813/.3—dc23

Broadview Press handles its own distribution in North America:
PO Box 1243, Peterborough, Ontario K9J 7H5, Canada
555 Riverwalk Parkway, Tonawanda, NY 14150, USA
Tel: (705) 743-8990; Fax: (705) 743-8353
email: customerservice@broadviewpress.com

For all territories outside of North America, distribution is handled by Eurospan Group.

Broadview Press acknowledges the financial support of the Government of Canada for our publishing activities.

Canadä

Developmental Editor: Laura Buzzard
Cover Designer: Lisa Brawn
Typesetter: Alexandria Stuart

PRINTED IN CANADA

Contents

Introduction

Martin R. Delany
1812 – 1885

Martin R. Delany's associate and rival Frederick Douglass once commented, "I thank God for making me a man simply; but Delany always thanks God for making him a *black man.*" One of the most powerful and provocative voices to emerge from the social and political unrest preceding the Civil War, the abolitionist and political activist Delany is today considered to have been among the earliest black nationalists. His career was extraordinarily wide-ranging—embracing the realms of journalism, medicine, the lecture and pamphlet-writing circuit, and the military—and his one published novel, *Blake* (1859, 1861–62), is often hailed as one of the masterpieces of nineteenth-century American literature. Delany provoked fiery disagreement as well as vehement admiration among the African American intellectual community, and his participation in some of the most important social debates of the mid-nineteenth century helped define the characteristics of the fight for black rights for decades to come.

Delany was born in Charles Town, Virginia (now West Virginia), to Pati and Samuel Delany, a free seamstress and an enslaved plantation worker. According to *partus* law, his mother's freedom was conferred upon him at birth; nevertheless, as Delany experienced throughout his life, the social and legal status of African Americans, whether free or enslaved, was constantly ambiguous and unstable. Pati was threatened with arrest in 1822 when it was found that her children had learned to read (Virginia prohibited the education of black people), and so fled with them northwards to Pennsylvania, where the family was joined by Samuel Delany once he had managed to purchase his freedom.

In 1831, at the age of nineteen, Delany moved to Pittsburgh to seek further education, and enrolled in a school associated with the African Methodist Episcopal (AME) Church. Here he started a literacy society, took up a medical apprenticeship (a career to which he would return at various stages throughout his life), attended black rights conventions, and engaged with black political leaders, including Lewis Woodson (who is sometimes described as the first black nationalist). In 1843 Delany founded the *Mystery*, an important African American newspaper. He dedicated the next several years of his life to this and related projects, before ceasing publication of the *Mystery* in 1847 to collaborate with Frederick Douglass on a new publication, the *North Star*. The *North Star* became very influential, but the collaboration was relatively brief. Douglass and Delany increasingly diverged in their approaches to abolitionism and black liberation, though they would continue to express respect for one another—sometimes begrudgingly—over the decades.

In November 1850, Delany was accepted into Harvard Medical School, and then promptly expelled following complaints from white students, who claimed that the admission of black classmates would damage the school's reputation (a smaller group of students counter-petitioned to let Delany remain, but Harvard faculty ignored this appeal). This personal humiliation proved something of a political catalyst for Delany, whose ideology became increasingly radical over the following years. The 1850s saw a number of regressive legislative decisions—beginning with the outrageous Fugitive Slave Act (1850)—that enraged the abolitionist community and confirmed the fears of many African Americans that the United States would never live up to its promises of democracy and equality. For Delany, the necessary resolution to the crisis was black emigration from the United States, and he put forward this view in *The Condition, Elevation, Emigration, and Destiny of the Colored People of the United States, Politically Considered* (1852). Two years later Delany sponsored the National Emigration Convention of Colored People in Cleveland, where he delivered an even more rousing address—published as *Political Destiny of the Colored Race on the American Continent* (1854)—calling on African Americans to recognize the profound oppression they faced in their country of birth and to respond by coming together to create a united, black-led nation of their own. At this point, Delany advocated emigration to South America; later he would change his focus to the African continent.

To Delany, it was essential to distinguish his plan from superficially similar projects that had been endorsed by various white political groups since earlier in the century. Most prominent was the white-led American Colonization Society, which had since 1821 encouraged thousands of free African Americans to migrate to the colony of Liberia. In Delany's view, Liberia was a "*burlesque* on government" that existed primarily to rid America of free African Americans and to ensure the continued enslavement of those who remained in bondage. (Historical records indicate, too, that the black colonists were often severely underfunded and insufficiently supported by their white American sponsors, which led to extreme mortality rates.)

Delany, by contrast, presented his plan as grounded in the pursuit of global black solidarity and liberation, and emphasized that the new nation he proposed would be governed by black leaders. Not everyone was convinced by the distinction, however. (Indeed, the text of *Political Destiny* was later used promotionally by white advocates of colonization.) Many black activists saw emigration as a betrayal of the struggle at home; in 1858 the Ohio Convention of Colored Men, under the leadership of William H. Day, resolved that "the amount of labor and self-sacrifice required to establish a home in a foreign land, would, if exercised here, redeem our native land from the grasp of slavery." Many others, however, did support Delany. African American priest James T. Holly, who would later settle in the Republic of Haiti, echoed Delany's ideas when he wrote that "[t]he social ostracism of the colored people in the United States is complete and irremediable. ... They must escape as Lot from the guilty and doomed cities of the plain, not even looking back upon this accursed land." Emigration remained a subject of heated debate among African Americans for decades, with Delany often at the center.

In 1856, Delany moved to Canada, where he set up a medical practice, wrote for Mary Ann Shadd Cary's abolitionist newspaper *The Provincial Freeman* (which advocated emigration to Canada), met with white militant abolitionist John Brown, and further developed his plans for emigration. In 1859, he traveled to west Africa, where he met with the Alake (King) of the Egba and agreed on a treaty that would grant land to African American immigrants (the Alake would, however, soon rescind his support, possibly under pressure from the British).

At the end of the decade Delany wrote his first and only novel, *Blake; or, the Huts of America* (serialized in 1859 and 1861–62; not published in book form until 1970), which tells the story of self-emancipated Henry Blake, who flees his plantation, travels through the South sowing the seeds of rebellion among the enslaved, leads his wife's family to freedom in Canada, and eventually travels to Cuba, where he plans a revolution of enslaved people. The book was written partly in response to Harriet Beecher Stowe's extraordinarily popular *Uncle Tom's Cabin* (1852), which Delany criticized for its failure to embrace black self-determination and its advocacy of Christian forbearance instead of direct action in response to the evils of slavery. *Blake* received little attention at the time of its publication—with its intended audience perhaps preoccupied by the Civil War—and even less in the following decades. The novel experienced a revival in 1970, however, when it was re-released in an edition that placed it in dialogue with the contemporary Black Power and Black Arts movements. Since then, *Blake* has become highly regarded by many critics, for whom the novel's revolutionary consciousness positions it as a counter to its more sentimental contemporaries (such as William Wells Brown's *Clotel*), and who celebrate its insistence on collective action and on the right of black people to demand liberation.

The progress of the Civil War marked a change of direction for Delany's efforts, as the struggle against slavery became militarized. Delany returned to the United States and began recruiting black soldiers for the Union Army, and in 1865, following an audience with President Abraham Lincoln, was made America's first black field major. After the end of the war, Delany continued to engage in American politics, running for lieutenant governor of South Carolina in 1874; he also wrote advice pamphlets intended for newly emancipated African Americans. In 1880, he resumed his medical practice in order to support his children; he continued this work until his death in 1885.

Delany remained a focus of debate as well as of admiration in the years following his death. AME bishop Daniel Payne wrote in

1888 that Delany had been "too intensely African to be popular," and lamented that his "love for his race" had been greater than his "love for humanity." Douglass put it more harshly: he claimed Delany had "gone about the same length in favor of black, as the whites have in favor of the doctrine of white supremacy." For others, however, the same qualities that disconcerted some of Delany's associates made him, as James Holly wrote, "one of the great men of this age." His legacy would only grow throughout the twentieth century, influencing writers such as W.E.B. Du Bois, as well as movements such as the Pan-Africanist movement.

Note on the Texts

The present volume, intended to offer a concise introduction to Delany's thought and writing, includes his important tract *Political Destiny of the Colored Race on the American Continent*, reproduced in full, followed by a substantial selection from his novel *Blake; or, the Huts of America*. The text of *Political Destiny* presented below is based on that appearing in *Proceedings of the National Emigration Convention of Colored People, held at Cleveland, Ohio, on Thursday, Friday and Saturday, the 24th, 25th and 26th of August, 1854*; the text of *Blake* is based on that published in *The Anglo-African Magazine* in 1859. Spelling and punctuation have been modernized according to the practices of *The Broadview Anthology of American Literature*.

CR

Political Destiny of the Colored Race on the American Continent

FELLOW COUNTRYMEN! The duty assigned us is an important one, comprehending all that pertains to our destiny and that of our posterity—present and prospectively. And while it must be admitted, that the subject is one of the greatest magnitude, requiring all that talents, prudence and wisdom might adduce, and while it would be folly to pretend to give you the combined result of these three agencies, we shall satisfy ourselves with doing our duty to the best of our ability, and that in the plainest, most simple and comprehensive manner.

Our object, then, shall be to place before you our true position in this country—the United States—the improbability of realizing our desires, and the sure, practicable and infallible remedy for the evils we now endure.

We have not addressed you as *citizens*—a term desired and ever cherished by us—because such you have never been. We have not addressed you as *freemen*—because such privileges have never been enjoyed by any colored man in the United States. Why then should we flatter your credulity, by inducing you to believe that which neither has now, nor never before had, an existence? Our oppressors are ever gratified at our manifest satisfaction, especially when that satisfaction is founded upon false premises; an assumption on our part, of the enjoyment of rights and privileges which never have been conceded, and which, according to the present system of the United States policy, we never can enjoy.

The *political policy* of this country was solely borrowed from, and shaped and modeled after, that of Rome. This was strikingly the case in the establishment of immunities, and the application of terms in their Civil and Legal regulations.

The term Citizen—politically considered—is derived from the Roman definition—which was never applied in any other sense— *Cives Ingenui*; which meant, one exempt from restraint of any kind. (*Cives*, a citizen; one who might enjoy the highest honors in his own free town—the town in which he lived—and in the country or commonwealth; and *Ingenui, freeborn*—of GOOD EXTRACTION.) All who were deprived of citizenship—that is, the right of enjoying positions of honor and trust—were termed *Hostes* and *Peregrini*; which are public and private *enemies*, and foreigners, or *aliens* to the country. (*Hostis*, a public—and sometimes—private enemy; and *Peregrinus*, an *alien, stranger, or foreigner.*)

The Romans, from a national pride, to distinguish their inhabitants from those of other countries, termed them all "citizens," but consequently, were under the necessity of specifying four classes of citizens: none but the *Cives Ingenui* being unrestricted in their privileges. There was one class, called the *Jus Quiritium*, or the wailing or *supplicating* citizen—that is, one who was continually *moaning, complaining*, or *crying for aid or succor*. This class might also include within themselves, the *jus suffragii*, who had the privilege of *voting*, but no other privilege. They could vote for one of their superiors— the *Cives Ingenui*—but not for themselves.

Such, then, is the condition, precisely, of the black and colored inhabitants of the United States; in some of the States they answering to the latter class, having the privilege of *voting*, to elevate their superiors to positions to which they need never dare aspire, or even hope to attain.

There has, of late years, been a false impression obtained, that the privilege of *voting* constitutes, or necessarily embodies, the *rights of citizenship*. A more radical error never obtained favor among an oppressed people. Suffrage is an ambiguous term, which admits of several definitions. But according to strict political construction, means simply "a vote, voice, approbation." Here, then, you have the whole import of the term suffrage. To have the "right of suffrage," as we rather proudly term it, is simply to have the *privilege*—there is no *right* about it—of giving our *approbation* to that which our *rulers may do*, without the privilege, on our part, of doing the same thing. Where such privileges are granted—privileges which are now exercised in but few of the States by colored men[1]—we have but the

---

1 *privileges which ... colored men* By 1854, only about 6 per cent of black men lived in states in which they could vote; these states were Maine, Massachusetts, Rhode Island, New Hampshire, Vermont, and, to a very limited degree, Wisconsin. Numerous other states had allowed some degree of black suffrage at certain points following the American Revolution,

privilege granted of saying, in common with others, who shall, for the time being, exercise *rights*, which, in him, are conceded to be *inherent* and *inviolate*. Like the indented[1] apprentice, who is summoned to give his approbation to an act which would be fully binding without his concurrence. Where there is no *acknowledged sovereignty*, there can be no binding power; hence, the suffrage of the black man, independently of the white, would be in this country unavailable.

Much might be adduced on this point to prove the insignificance of the black man, politically considered in this country, but we deem it wholly unnecessary at present, and consequently proceed at once to consider another feature of this important subject.

Let it then be understood, as a great principle of political economy, that no people can be free who themselves do not constitute an essential part of the *ruling element* of the country in which they live. Whether this element be founded upon a true or false, a just or an unjust basis; this position in community is necessary to personal safety. The liberty of no man is secure, who controls not his own political destiny. What is true of an individual, is true of a family; and that which is true of a family, is also true concerning a whole people. To suppose otherwise, is that delusion which at once induces its victim, through a period of long suffering, patiently to submit to every species of wrong; trusting against probability, and hoping against all reasonable grounds of expectation, for the granting of privileges and enjoyment of rights, which never will be attained. This delusion reveals the true secret of the power which holds in peaceable subjection, all the oppressed in every part of the world.

A people, to be free, must necessarily be *their own rulers*: that is, *each individual* must, in himself, embody the *essential ingredient*—so to speak—of the *sovereign principle* which composes the *true basis* of his liberty. This principle, when not exercised by himself, may, at his pleasure, be delegated to another—his true representative.

---

but in all these states the right was later rescinded. Even where black men could legally vote, harsh discrimination and violence often prevented them from exercising their right.

1   *indented* Indentured. Indentured servants and apprentices were bound to work without pay for a fixed period of time. Such indentures were usually at least somewhat voluntary, but the contracts were often liable to be sold to different employers with little to no consultation with the servant or apprentice in question.

Said a great French writer:[1] "A free agent, in a free government, should be his own governor"; that is, he must possess within himself the *acknowledged right to govern*: this constitutes him a *governor*, though he may delegate to another the power to govern himself. No one, then, can delegate to another a power he never possessed; that is, he cannot *give an agency* in that which he never had a right. Consequently, the colored man in the United States, being deprived of the right of inherent sovereignty, cannot *confer* a suffrage, because he possesses none to confer. Therefore, where there is no suffrage, there can be neither *freedom* nor *safety* for the disfranchised. And it is a futile hope to suppose that the agent of another's concerns will take a proper interest in the affairs of those to whom he is under no obligations. Having no favors to ask or expect, he therefore has none to lose.

In other periods and parts of the world—as in Europe and Asia—the people being of one common, direct origin of race, though established on the presumption of difference by birth, or what was termed *blood*, yet the distinction between the superior classes and common people, could only be marked by the difference in the dress and education of the two classes. To effect this, the interposition of government was necessary; consequently, the costume and education of the people became a subject of legal restriction, guarding carefully against the privileges of the common people.

In Rome, the Patrician and Plebian were orders in the ranks of her people—all of whom were termed citizens (*cives*)—recognized by the laws of the country; their dress and education being determined by law, the better to fix the distinction. In different parts of Europe, at the present day, if not the same, the distinction among the people is similar, only on a modified—and in some kingdoms—probably more tolerant or deceptive policy.

In the United States, our degradation being once—as it has in a hundred instances been done—legally determined, our color is sufficient, independently of costume, education, or other distinguishing marks, to keep up that distinction.

In Europe, when an inferior is elevated to the rank of equality with the superior class, the law first comes to his aid, which, in its decrees,

---

1   *great French writer*   Probably alluding to *Principles of Politics* (1815) by Swiss-French political philosopher Benjamin Constant.

entirely destroys his identity as an inferior, leaving no trace of his former condition visible.

In the United States, among the whites, their color is made, by law and custom, the mark of distinction and superiority; while the color of the blacks is a badge of degradation, acknowledged by statute, organic law,[1] and the common consent of the people.

With this view of the case—which we hold to be correct—to elevate to equality the degraded subject of law and custom, it can only be done, as in Europe, by an entire destruction of the identity of the former condition of the applicant. Even were this desirable—which we by no means admit—with the deep seated prejudices engendered by oppression, with which we have to contend, ages incalculable might reasonably be expected to roll around, before this could honorably be accomplished; otherwise, we should encourage and at once commence an indiscriminate concubinage and immoral commerce, of our mothers, sisters, wives and daughters, revolting to think of, and a physical curse to humanity.

If this state of things be to succeed, then, as in Egypt, under the dread of the inscrutable approach of the destroying angel, to appease the hatred of our oppressors, as a license to the passions of every white, let the lintel of each door of every black man, be stained with the blood of virgin purity and unsullied matron fidelity. Let it be written along the cornice in capitals, "The *will* of the white man is the rule of my household."[2] Remove the protection to our chambers and nurseries, that the places once sacred, may henceforth become the unrestrained resort of the vagrant and rabble, always provided that the licensed commissioner of lust shall wear the indisputable impress of a *white* skin.

But we have fully discovered and comprehended the great political disease with which we are affected, the cause of its origin and continuance; and what is now left for us to do, is to discover and apply a sovereign remedy—a healing balm to a sorely diseased body—a wrecked but not entirely shattered system. We propose for this disease

---

1   *organic law* Foundational law or legal structure of a nation.

2   *as in Egypt … my household* Allusion to the Book of Exodus, which tells the story of the Israelites' escape from enslavement in Egypt. In Exodus 12.21–23, Moses tells the Israelites to mark the lintels of their doors with lambs' blood so that God will know not to smite them when bringing destruction upon the Egyptians.

a remedy. That remedy is Emigration. This Emigration should be well advised, and like remedies applied to remove the disease from the physical system of man, skillfully and carefully applied, within the proper time, directed to operate on that part of the system, whose greatest tendency shall be to benefit the whole.

Several geographical localities have been named, among which rank the Canadas.[1] These we do not object to as places of temporary relief, especially to the fleeing fugitive[2]—which, like a palliative, soothes for the time being the misery—but cannot commend them as permanent places upon which to fix our destiny, and that of our children, who shall come after us. But in this connexion, we would most earnestly recommend to the colored people of the United States generally, to secure by purchase all of the land they possibly can, while selling at low rates, under the British people and government. As that time may come, when, like the lands in the United States territories generally, if not as in Oregon and some other territories and States, they may be prevented entirely from settling or purchasing them—the preference being given to the white applicant.

And here, we would not deceive you by disguising the facts, that according to political tendency, the Canadas—as all British America—at no very distant day, are destined to come into the United States.

And were this not the case, the odds are against us, because the ruling element there, as in the United States, is, and ever must be, white—the population now standing, in all British America, two and a half millions of whites, to but forty thousand of the black race; or sixty-one and a fraction whites to one black!—the difference being eleven times greater than in the United States—so that colored people might never hope for anything more than to exist politically by mere sufferance—occupying a secondary position to the white of the Canadas. The Yankees from this side of the lakes, are fast settling in the Canadas, infusing, with industrious success, all the malignity and

---

1 *the Canadas* At this period in history, the Province of Canada largely comprised present-day Ontario and Quebec; until 1841 these were considered separately as Upper and Lower Canada, leading to the collective term "the Canadas."

2 *fleeing fugitive* Following the notorious 1850 Fugitive Slave Act, free people in the North and South were required by law to aid in the capture of fugitives, making even free states unsafe for those escaping slavery.

negro-hate, inseparable from their very being, as Christian Democrats and American advocates of equality.

Then, to be successful, our attention must be turned in a direction towards those places where the black and colored man comprise, by population, and constitute by necessity of numbers, the *ruling element* of the body politic. And where, when occasion shall require it, the issue can be made and maintained on this basis. Where our political enclosure and national edifice can be reared, established, walled, and proudly defended on this great elementary principle of original identity. Upon this solid foundation rests the fabric of every substantial political structure in the world, which cannot exist without it; and so soon as a people or nation lose their original identity, just so soon must that nation or people become extinct. Powerful though they may have been, they must fall. Because the nucleus which heretofore held them together, becoming extinct, there being no longer a centre of attraction, or basis for a union of the parts, a dissolution must as naturally ensue, as the result of the neutrality of the basis of adhesion among the particles of matter.

This is the secret of the eventful downfall of Egypt, Carthage, Rome, and the former Grecian States, once so powerful—a loss of original identity; and with it, a loss of interest in maintaining their fundamental principles of nationality.

This, also, is the great secret of the present strength of Great Britain, Russia, the United States, and Turkey; and the endurance of the French nation, whatever its strength and power, is attributable only to their identity as Frenchmen.

And doubtless the downfall of Hungary, brave and noble as may be her people, is mainly to be attributed to the want of identity of origin, and, consequently, a union of interests and purpose. This fact it might not have been expected would be admitted by the great Magyar,[1] in his thrilling pleas for the restoration of Hungary, when asking aid,

---

1   *great Magyar*   Hungarian political leader Lajos Kossuth, who ruled a short-lived Kingdom of Hungary (1848–49) after declaring it free from Austrian rule. In the United States, Kossuth was both hailed as a revolutionary freedom fighter and, later, criticized for his refusal to condemn slavery; *Magyar* Hungarian.

both national and individual, to enable him to throw off the ponder-ous weight placed upon their shoulders by the House of Hapsburg.[1]

Hungary consisted of three distinct "races"—as they called them-selves—of people, all priding in and claiming rights based on their originality—the Magyars, Celts, and Slavs. On the encroachment of Austria, each one of these races—declaring for nationality—rose up against the House of Hapsburg, claiming the right of self-govern-ment, premised on their origin. Between the three a compromise was effected—the Magyars, being the majority, claimed the precedence. They made an effort, but for the want of a unity of interests—an identity of origin—the noble Hungarians failed. All know the result.

Nor is this the only important consideration. Were we content to remain as we are, sparsely interspersed among our white fellow-countrymen, we never might be expected to equal them in any honorable or respectable competition for a livelihood. For the reason that, according to the customs and policy of the country, we for ages would be kept in a secondary position, every situation of respectabil-ity, honor, profit or trust, either as mechanics, clerks, teachers, jurors, councilmen, or legislators, being filled by white men, consequently, our energies must become paralyzed or enervated for the want of proper encouragement.

This example upon our children, and the colored people gener-ally, is pernicious and degrading in the extreme. And how could it otherwise be, when they see every place of respectability filled and occupied by the whites, they pandering to their vanity, and existing among them merely as a thing of conveniency?

Our friends in this and other countries, anxious for our elevation, have for years been erroneously urging us to lose our identity as a distinct race, declaring that we were the same as other people; while at the very same time their own representative was traversing the world and propagating the doctrine in favor of a *universal Anglo-Saxon predominance*. The "Universal Brotherhood," so able and eloquently advocated by that Polyglot Christian Apostle[2] of this doctrine, had

---

1   *House of Hapsburg*   The ruling royal house of the Austrian Empire (by this point in history officially titled the House of Habsburg-Lorraine).

2   [Delany's note]   Elihu Burritt. [The famously multilingual Burritt was an abolitionist and advocate of global peace who founded the pacifist League of Universal Brotherhood in 1846. Though Burritt's own perspectives on race were relatively progressive for a white intel-

established as its basis, a universal acknowledgement of the Anglo-Saxon rule.

The truth is, we are not identical with the Anglo-Saxon or any other race of the Caucasian or pure white type of the human family, and the sooner we know and acknowledge this truth, the better for ourselves and posterity.

The English, French, Irish, German, Italian, Turk, Persian, Greek, Jew, and all other races, have their native or inherent peculiarities, and why not our race? We are not willing, therefore, at all times and under all circumstances to be moulded into various shapes of eccentricity, to suit the caprices and conveniences of every kind of people. We are not more suitable to everybody than everybody is suitable to us; therefore, no more like other people than others are like us.

We have then inherent traits, attributes—so to speak—and native characteristics, peculiar to our race—whether pure or mixed blood—and all that is required of us is to cultivate these and develop them in their purity, to make them desirable and emulated by the rest of the world.

That the colored races have the highest traits of civilization, will not be disputed. They are civil, peaceable and religious to a fault. In mathematics, sculpture and architecture, as arts and sciences, commerce and internal improvements as enterprises, the white race may probably excel; but in languages, oratory, poetry, music and painting as arts and sciences, and in ethics, metaphysics, theology and legal jurisprudence; in plain language—in the true principles of morals, correctness of thought, religion, and law or civil government, there is no doubt but the black race will yet instruct the world.

It would be duplicity longer to disguise the fact, that the great issue, sooner or later, upon which must be disputed the world's destiny, will be a question of black and white; and every individual will be called upon for his identity with one or the other. The blacks and colored races are four-sixths of all the population of the world; and these people are fast tending to a common cause with each other. The white races are but one-third of the population of the globe—or one of them to two of us—and it cannot much longer continue, that

<hr>

lectual of his era, Delany expresses frustration with the League's view that racial differences should be ignored. Most of the League's leading members were white, and Burritt focused disproportionately on Britain and Ireland in his advocacy of international "brotherhood."]

two-thirds will passively submit to the universal domination of this one-third. And it is notorious that the only progress made in territorial domain, in the last three centuries, by the whites, has been a usurpation and encroachment on the rights and native soil of some of the colored races.

The East Indies, Java, Sumatra, the Azores, Madeira, Canary, and Cape Verde Islands; Socotra, Guardifui and the Isle of France; Algiers, Tunis, Tripoli, Barca and Egypt in the North, Sierra Leone in the West, and Cape Colony in the South of Africa;[1] besides many other Islands and possessions not herein named. Australia, the Ladrone Islands,[2] together with many others of Oceanica; the seizure and appropriation of a great portion of the Western Continent, with all its Islands, were so many encroachments of the whites upon the rights of the colored races. Nor are they yet content, but, intoxicated with the success of their career, the Sandwich Islands[3] are now marked out as the next booty to be seized, in the ravages of their exterminating crusade.

We regret the necessity of stating the fact—but duty compels us to the task—that for more than two thousand years, the determined aim of the whites has been to crush the colored races wherever found. With a determined will, they have sought and pursued them in every quarter of the globe. The Anglo-Saxon has taken the lead in this work of universal subjugation. But the Anglo-American stands pre-eminent for deeds of injustice and acts of oppression, unparalleled perhaps in the annals of modern history.

We admit the existence of great and good people in America, England, France, and the rest of Europe, who desire a unity of interests among the whole human family, of whatever origin or race.

---

1 *The East Indies ... Africa* At the time of Delany's writing, the places named here were colonies under European, Arabic, or Ottoman rule. Though many of the Atlantic island colonies had been uninhabited at the time of colonization, they became crucial centers of the transatlantic slave trade; *Socotra* Island in the Indian Ocean, now part of Yemen; *Guardifui* Cape at the tip of what is now Somalia; *Isle of France* What is now the island nation of Mauritius; *Barca* Also known as Cyrenaica, a coastal region in what is now Libya.

2 *Ladrone Islands* The Mariana Islands, today comprising two territories of the United States.

3 *Sandwich Islands* Now known as the Hawaiian Islands (formerly named after the British Earl of Sandwich).

But it is neither the moralist, Christian, nor philanthropist whom we now have to meet and combat, but the politician—the civil engineer and skillful economist—who direct and control the machinery which moves forward with mighty impulse, the nations and powers of the earth. We must, therefore, if possible, meet them on vantage ground, or, at least, with adequate means for the conflict.

Should we encounter an enemy with artillery, a prayer will not stay the cannon shot; neither will the kind words nor smiles of philanthropy shield his spear from piercing us through the heart. We must meet mankind, then, as they meet us—prepared for the worst, though we may hope for the best. Our submission does not gain for us an increase of friends nor respectability—as the white race will only respect those who oppose their usurpation, and acknowledge as equals those who will not submit to their rule. This may be no new discovery in political economy, but it certainly is a subject worthy the consideration of the black race.

After a due consideration of these facts, as herein recounted, shall we stand still and continue inactive—the passive observers of the great events of the times and age in which we live; submitting indifferently to the usurpation, by the white race, of every right belonging to the blacks? Shall the last vestige of an opportunity, outside of the continent of Africa, for the national development of our race, be permitted, in consequence of our slothfulness, to elude our grasp and fall into the possession of the whites? This, may Heaven forbid. May the sturdy, intelligent Africo-American sons of the Western Continent forbid.

Longer to remain inactive, it should be borne in mind, may be to give an opportunity to despoil us of every right and possession sacred to our existence, with which God has endowed us as a heritage on the earth. For let it not be forgotten, that the white race—who numbers but *one* of them to *two* of us—originally located in Europe, besides possessing all of that continent, have now got hold of a large portion of Asia, Africa, all North America, a portion of South America, and all of the great Islands of both Hemispheres, except Paupau, or New Guinea, inhabited by negroes and Malays, in Oceanica; the Japanese Islands, peopled and ruled by the Japanese; Madagascar, peopled by negroes, near the coast of Africa; and the Island of Haiti, in the West Indies, peopled by as brave and noble descendants of Africa, as they who laid the foundation of Thebias,[1] or constructed the everlasting pyramids and catacombs of Egypt. A people who have freed themselves by the might of their own will, the force of their own power, the unfailing strength of their own right arms, and their unflinching determination to be free.[2]

Let us, then, not survive the disgrace and ordeal of Almighty displeasure, of two to one, witnessing the universal possession and control by the whites, of every habitable portion of the earth. For such must inevitably be the case, and that, too, at no distant day, if black men do not take advantage of the opportunity, by grasping hold of those places where chance is in their favor, and establishing the rights and power of the colored race.

We must make an issue, create an event, and establish for ourselves a position. This is essentially necessary for our effective elevation as a people, in shaping our national development, directing our destiny, and redeeming ourselves as a race.

If we but determine it shall be so, it *will* be so; and there is nothing under the sun can prevent it. We shall then be but in pursuit of our legitimate claims to inherent rights, bequeathed to us by the will of Heaven—the endowment of God, our common parent. A distinguished economist has truly said, "God has implanted in man an infinite progression in the career of improvement. A soul capacitated for improvement ought not to be bounded by a tyrant's landmarks."[3] This sentiment is just and true, the application of which to our case, is adapted with singular fitness.

Having glanced hastily at our present political position in the world generally, and the United States in particular—the fundamental disadvantages under which we exist, and the improbability of ever

---

1   *Thebias* Thebes, ancient Egyptian city.

2   *Island of Haiti ... to be free* The Haitian Revolution began in August 1791, when thousands of enslaved people under the leadership of the formerly enslaved Toussaint L'Ouverture rebelled against the white planter class and took over the island then known as Saint-Domingue. By 1804, the French colonial government had been overthrown and the elective Empire of Haiti, led by formerly enslaved Jean-Jacques Dessalines, had been established. The violent means taken to secure Haiti's independence were controversial even among abolitionists, but the success of the Revolution was inspirational to many abolitionists and black leaders throughout the nineteenth century.

3   *God has ... tyrant's landmarks* Paraphrased from *The Revelation of Rights* (1841) by Elias E. Ellmaker, a Pennsylvanian lawyer and fierce advocate against slavery and other forms of tyranny.

attaining citizenship and equality of rights in this country—we call your attention next, to the places of destination to which we shall direct Emigration.

The West Indies, Central and South America, are the countries of our choice, the advantages of which shall be made apparent to your entire satisfaction.

Though we have designated them as countries, they are in fact but one country—relatively considered—a part of this, the Western Continent.

As now politically divided, they consist of the following classification—each group or division placed under its proper national head:

	FRENCH ISLANDS	
Consist of:	Square miles.	Population in 1840
Guadeloupe,	675	124,000
Martinico,	260	110,000
St. Martin, N. part,	15	6,000
Mariegalante,	90	11,500
Deseada,	25	1,500

	DANISH ISLANDS	
Santa Cruz,	80	34,000
St. Thomas,	50	15,000
St. Johns,	70	3,000

	SWEDISH	
St. Bartholomew,	25	8,000

	DUTCH	
St. Eustatia,	10	20,000
Curacoa,	375	12,000
St. Martin, S. part,	10	5,000
Saba,	20	9,000

	VENEZUELA	
Consist of:	Square miles.	Population in 1840
Margarita,	00[1]	16,000

	SPANISH	
Cuba,	43,500	725,000
Porto Rico,	4,000	325,000

	BRITISH	
Jamaica,	5,520	375,000
Barbadoes,	164	102,000
Trinidad,	1,970	45,000
Antigua,	108	36,000
Grenada and the Granadines,	120	29,000
St. Vincent,	121	36,000
St. Kitts,	68	24,000
Dominica,	275	20,000
St. Lucia,	275	18,000
Tobago,	120	14,000
Nevis,	20	12,000
Montserat,	47	8,000
Tortola,	20	7,000
Barbuda,	72	0,000
Anguilla,	90	3,000
Bahamas,	4,440	18,000
Bermudas,	20	10,000

	HAITIAN NATION	
Haiti,	000	800,000

In addition to these, there are a number of smaller Islands, belonging to the Little Antilles, the area and population of which are not known, many of them being unpopulated.

These Islands, in the aggregate, form an area—allowing 40,000 square miles to Haiti and her adjunct islands, and something for those the statistics of which are unknown—of about 103,000, or equal in extent to Rhode Island, New York, New Jersey and Pennsylvania, and

---

1　*00*　The zeroes found in several sections of the table appear to indicate regions for which statistics were unavailable.

little less than the United Kingdoms of England, Scotland, Ireland and the principality of Wales.

The population being on the above date, 1840: 3,115,000—three millions, one hundred and fifteen thousand—and allowing an increase of *ten per cent* in ten years, on the entire population, there are now 3,250,000 (three millions, two hundred and fifty thousand) inhabitants, who comprise the people of these islands.

CENTRAL AMERICA

Consists of—	Population in 1840
Guatemala,	800,000
San Salvador,	350,000
Honduras,	250,000
Costa Rica,	150,000
Nicaragua,	250,000

These consist of five States, as shown in the above statistics, the united population of which, in 1840, amounted to 1,800,000 (one million, eight hundred thousand) inhabitants. The number at present being estimated at 2,500,000 (two and a half millions) shows, in thirteen years, 700,000 (seven hundred thousand), being one-third and one-eighteenth of an increase in population.

SOUTH AMERICA

Consists of—	Square miles.	Population in 1840.
New Grenada,	450,000	1,687,000
Venezuela,	420,000	900,000
Ecuador,	280,000	600,000
Guiana,	160,000	182,000
Brazil,	3,390,000	5,000,000
North Peru,	300,000	700,000
South Peru,	130,000	800,000
Bolivia,	450,000	1,716,000
Buenos Ayres,	750,00	700,000
Paraguay,	88,000	150,000
Uruguay,	92,000	75,000
Chili,	170,000	1,500,000
Patagonia,	370,00	30,000

The total area of these States is 7,050,000 (seven millions and fifty thousand) square miles; but comparatively little (450,000 square miles), less than the whole area of North America, in which we live.

But one State in South America—Brazil—is an abject slave-holding State;[1] and even here, all free men are socially and politically equal, negroes and colored men partly of African descent, holding offices of honor, trust and rank, without restriction. In the other States, slavery is not known, all the inhabitants enjoying political equality, restrictions on account of color being entirely unknown, unless, indeed, necessity induces it, when, in all such cases, the preference is given to the colored man, to put a check to European presumption, and insufferable Yankee intrusion and impudence.

The aggregate population was 14,040,000 (fourteen millions and forty thousand) in 1840. Allowing for thirteen years the same ratio of increase as that of the Central American States—being one-third (4,680,000)—and this gives at present a population of 18,720,000 in South America.

Add to this the population of the Antilles and Guatemala, and this gives a population in the West Indies, Central and South America of 24,470,000 (twenty-four millions, four hundred seventy thousand) inhabitants.

But one-seventh of this population, 3,495,714, (three millions, four hundred and ninety-five thousand, seven hundred and fourteen) being white, or of pure European extraction, there is a population throughout this vast area of 20,974,286 (twenty millions, nine hundred and seventy-four thousand, two hundred and eighty-six) colored persons, who constitute, from the immense preponderance of their numbers, the *ruling element*, as they ever must be, of those countries.

There are no influences that could be brought to bear to change this most fortunate and Heaven-designed state and condition of things. Nature here has done her own work, which the art of knaves nor the schemes of deep-designing political impostors can never reach. This is a fixed fact in the zodiac of the political heavens, that the blacks and colored people are the stars which must ever most conspicuously twinkle in the firmament of this division of the Western Hemisphere.

---

1   *abject slave-holding State*   Brazil was the last western nation to legally abolish slavery, in 1888.

We next invite your attention to a few facts, upon which we predicate the claims of the black race, not only to the tropical regions and *South temperate zone* of this hemisphere, but to the whole Continent, North as well as South. And here we desire it distinctly to be understood, that, in the selection of our places of destination, we do not advocate the *Southern* scheme as a concession, nor yet at the will nor desire of our North American oppressors; but as a policy, by which we must be the greatest political gainers, without the risk or possibility of loss to ourselves. A gain by which the lever of political elevation and machinery of national progress must ever be held and directed by our own hands and heads, to our own will and purposes, in defiance of the obstructions which might be attempted on the part of a dangerous and deep-designing oppressor.

From the year 1492, the discovery of Hispaniola—the first land discovered by Columbus in the New World—to 1502, the short space of ten years, such was the mortality among the natives, that the Spaniards, then holding rule there, "began to employ a few"[1] Africans in the mines of the Island. The experiment was effective—a successful one. The Indian and the African were enslaved together, when the Indian sunk, and the African stood.

It was not until June the 24th, of the year 1498, that the Continent was discovered by John Cabot,[2] a Venetian, who sailed in August of the previous year, 1497, from Bristol, under the patronage of Henry the VII, King of England.

In 1517, the short space of but fifteen years from the date of their introduction, Carolus V, King of Spain, by right of a patent, granted permission to a number of persons annually to supply the islands of Hispaniola (St. Domingo[3]), Cuba, Jamaica and Porto Rico, with natives of Africa, to the number of four thousand annually. John

---

1   *began to employ a few*   The quoted phrasing is used in *The History, Civil and Commercial, of the West Indies* (1793) by English proslavery politician Bryan Edwards.

2   *John Cabot*   Giovanni Caboto (c. 1450–c. 1500), a Venetian who explored the coast of North America.

3   *Hispaniola (St. Domingo)*   Hispaniola is the name of the island that once held the French colony of Saint-Domingue (now Haiti) and the Spanish colony of what is now the Dominican Republic.

Hawkins,[1] a mercenary Englishman, was the first person known to engage in this general system of debasing our race, and his royal mistress, Queen Elizabeth, was engaged with him in interest and shared the general profits.

The Africans, on their advent into a foreign country, soon experienced the want of their accustomed food, and habits and manner of living.

The aborigines subsisted mainly by game and fish, with a few patches of maize, or Indian corn, near their wigwams, which were generally attended by the women, while the men were absent engaged in the chase, or at war with a hostile tribe. The vegetables, grains and fruits, such as in their native country they had been accustomed to, were not to be obtained among the aborigines, which first induced the African laborer to cultivate "patches" of ground in the neighborhood of the mining operations, for the purpose of raising food for his own sustenance.

This trait in their character was observed and regarded with considerable interest; after which the Spaniards and other colonists, on contracting with the English slave dealers—Captain Hawkins and others—for new supplies of slaves, were careful to request that an adequate quantity of seeds and plants of various kinds, indigenous to the continent of Africa, especially those composing the staple products of the natives, be selected and brought out with the slaves to the New World. Many of these were cultivated to a considerable extent, while those indigenous to America were cultivated with great success.

Shortly after the commencement of the slave trade, under Elizabeth and Hawkins, the Queen granted a license to Sir Walter Raleigh[2] to search for uninhabited lands, and seize upon all unoccupied by Christians. Sir Walter discovered the coast of North Carolina and Virginia, assigning the name "Virginia" to the whole coast now comprising the old Thirteen States.

---

1   *John Hawkins*   English naval commander (1532–95) and reputedly the first English person to profit from the Atlantic slave trade, who led expeditions to West Africa in order to kidnap and enslave people there.
2   *Sir Walter Raleigh*   English explorer and poet (c. 1552–1618), known as a favorite of Queen Elizabeth I who granted him a royal charter to explore and colonize any "remote, heathen and barbarous lands" he could find.

A feeble colony was here settled, which did not avail much, and it was not until the month of April, 1607, that the first permanent settlement was made in Virginia, under the patronage of letters patent from James I, King of England, to Thomas Gates and associates. This was the first settlement of North America, and thirteen years anterior to the landing of the Pilgrims on Plymouth Rock.

And we shall now introduce to you, from acknowledged authority, a number of historical extracts, to prove that previous to the introduction of the black race upon this continent, but little enterprise of any kind was successfully carried on. The African or negro was the first *available contributor* to the country, and consequently is by priority of right, and politically should be, entitled to the highest claims of an eligible citizen.

"No permanent settlement was effected in what is now called the United States, till the reign of James the First."—*Ramsay's Hist. U.S.*,[1] Vol. 1. p. 38.

"The month of April, 1607, is the epoch of the first permanent settlement on the coast of Virginia, the name then given to all that extent of country which forms thirteen States."—*Ib.* p. 39.

The whole coast of the country was at this time explored, not for the purpose of trade and agriculture—because there were then no such enterprises in the country, the natives not producing sufficient of the necessaries of life, to supply present wants, there being consequently nothing to trade for—but, like their Spanish and Portuguese predecessors, who occupied the Islands and different parts of South America, in search of gold and other precious metals.

Trade and the cultivation of the soil, on coming to the new world, were foreign to their intention or designs, consequently, when failing of success in that enterprise, they were sadly disappointed.

"At a time when the precious metals were conceived to be the peculiar and only valuable productions of the new world, when every mountain was supposed to contain a treasure, and every rivulet was searched for its golden sands, this appearance was fondly considered as an infallible indication of the mine. Every hand was eager to dig. * * *

---

1   *Ramsay's Hist. U.S.* The following quotations are from Davis Ramsay's *History of the United States, from the First Settlement as English Colonies, in 1607, to the Year 1808* (1816).

"'There was now,' says Smith,[1] 'no talk, no hope, no work; but dig gold, wash gold, refine gold.' With this imaginary wealth, the first vessel returning to England was loaded, while the *culture of the land* and every useful occupation was *totally neglected*.

"The colonists thus left, were in miserable circumstances for want of provisions. The remainder of what they had brought with them was so small in quantity, as to be soon expended—and so damaged, in course of a long voyage, as to be a source of disease.

" * * In their expectation of getting gold, the people were disappointed, the glittering substance they had sent to England, proving to be a valueless mineral. Smith, on his return to Jamestown, found the colony reduced to thirty-eight persons, who, in despair, were preparing to abandon the country. He employed caresses, threats, and even violence, in order to prevent them from executing this fatal resolution."—*Ibid*, pp. 45–6.

The Pilgrims or Puritans, in November 1620, after having organized with solemn vows to the defence of each other, and the maintenance of their civil liberty, made the harbor of Cape Cod, landing safely on "Plymouth Rock," December 20th, about one month subsequently. They were one hundred and one in number, and from the *toils* and *hardships* consequent to a *severe season*, in a *strange country*, in less than six months after their arrival, "forty persons—nearly one-half of their original number"—had died.

"In 1618, in the reign of James I, the British government established a regular trade on the coast of Africa. In the year 1620, negro slaves began to be imported into Virginia; a Dutch ship bringing twenty of them for sale."—*Sampson's Historical Dictionary*,[2] p. 348.

It will be seen by these historical reminiscences, that the Dutch ship landed her cargo at New Bedford, Massachusetts—the whole coast now comprising the old original States, then went by the name of Virginia, being so named by Sir Walter Raleigh, in honor of his royal mistress and patron, Elizabeth, the Virgin Queen of England,

---

1 *Smith* English explorer John Smith, a leader in the establishment of the Jamestown colony in Virginia who wrote numerous reports of the settlement, including *The Proceedings of the English Colony in Virginia* (1612), which Ramsay quotes here.

2 *Sampson's Historical Dictionary* From American chaplain Ezra Sampson's *The Youth's Companion, or an Historical Dictionary* (1813).

under whom he received the patent of his royal commission, to seize all the lands unoccupied by Christians.

Beginning their preparations in the slave trade in 1618, just two years previous—allowing time against the landing of the first emigrants, for successfully carrying out the project—the African captives and Puritan emigrants—singularly enough!—landed upon the same section of the continent at the same time—1620—the Pilgrims at Plymouth, and the captive slaves at New Bedford, but a few miles, comparatively, South.

"The country at this period, was one vast wilderness. The continent of North America was then one continued forest. * *

"There were no horses, cattle, sheep, hogs, or tame beasts of any kind. * * There were no domestic poultry. * * There were no gardens, orchards, public roads, meadows, or cultivated fields.— * * They often burned the woods that they could advantageously plant their corn. * *

"They had neither spice, salt, bread, butter, cheese, nor milk.— They had no set meals, but eat[1] when they were hungry, or could find anything to satisfy the cravings of nature.

"Very little of their food was derived from the earth, except what it spontaneously produced. * * The ground was both their seat and table. * * Their best bed was a skin. * * They had neither iron, steel, nor any metallic instruments."—*Ramsay's Hist.*, pp. 39–40.

We adduce not these extracts to disparage or detract from the real worth of our brother Indian—for we are identical as the subjects of American wrongs, outrages, and oppression; and therefore one in interest—far be it from our designs. Whatever opinion he may entertain of our race—in accordance with the impressions made by the contumely heaped upon us by our mutual oppressor, the American nation—we admire his, for the many deeds of heroic and noble daring with which the brief history of his liberty-loving people is replete. We sympathise with him, because our brethren are the successors of his, in the degradation of American bondage; and we adduce them in evidence against the many aspersions heaped upon the African race, avowing that their inferiority to the other races, and unfitness for a high civil and social position, caused them to be reduced to servitude.

---

1   *eat*   Ate.

For the purpose of proving their availability and eminent fitness alone—not to say superiority—and not inferiority, first suggested to Europeans the substitution of African for that of Indian labor in the mines; that their superior adaptation to the difficulties consequent to a new country and different climate, made them preferable to Europeans themselves; and their superior skill, industry, and general thriftiness in all that they did, first suggested to the colonists the propriety of turning their attention to agricultural and other industrial pursuits than those of mining operations.

It is evident, from what has herein been adduced—the settlement of Capt. John Smith being in the course of a few months, reduced to thirty-eight, and that of the Pilgrims at Plymoth, from one hundred and one, to fifty-seven, in six months—that the whites nor aborigines were equal to the hard, and to them insurmountable difficulties, which then stood wide-spread before them.

An endless forest—the impenetrable earth—the one to be removed and the other to be excavated. Towns and cities to be built, and farms to be cultivated: all presented difficulties too arduous for the European then here, and entirely unknown to the native of the continent.

At a period such as this, when the natives themselves had fallen victims to the tasks imposed upon them by the usurpers, and the Europeans also were fast sinking beneath the influence and weight of climate and hardships; when food could not be obtained, nor the common conveniences of life procured; when arduous duties of life were to be performed, and none capable of doing them—save those who had previously by their labors, not only in their own country, but in the new, so proven themselves capable—it is very evident, as the most natural consequence, the Africans were resorted to, for the performance of every duty common to domestic life.

There were no laborers known to the Colonists, from Cape Cod to Cape Lookout,[1] than those of the African race. They entered at once into the mines, extracting therefrom the rich treasures which for a thousand ages lay hidden in the earth; when plunging into the depths of the rivers, they culled from their sandy bottoms, to the astonishment of the natives and surprise of the Europeans, minerals

---

1 *Cape Cod to Cape Lookout* In Massachusetts and North Carolina, respectively.

and precious stones, which added to the pride and aggrandisement of every throne in Europe.

And from their knowledge of cultivation—an art acquired in their native Africa—the farming interests in the North and planting in the South, were commenced with a prospect never dreamed of before the introduction on the continent of this most interesting, unexampled, hardy race of men. A race capable of the endurance of more toil, fatigue and hunger, than any other branch of the human family.

Though pagans for the most part in their own country, they required not to be taught to work, and how to do it; but it was only necessary to bid them work, and they at once knew what to do, and how it should be done.

Even up to the present day, it is notorious that in the planting States,[1] the blacks themselves are the only skillful cultivators of the soil, the proprietors or planters, as they are termed, knowing little or nothing of the art, save that which they learn from the African husbandman;[2] while the ignorant white overseer, whose duty is to see that the work is attended to, knows still less.

Hemp, cotton, tobacco, corn, rice, sugar, and many other important staple products, are all the result of African skill and labor, in the southern States of this country. The greater number of the mechanics of the South are also black men.

Nor was their skill as herdsmen inferior to their other proficiencies, they being among the most accomplished trainers of horses in the world.

Indeed, to this class of men may be indebted the entire country, for the improvement [in the] South, in the breed of horses. And those who have traveled in the southern States could not have failed to observe that the principal trainers, jockeys, riders, and judges of horses, were men of African descent.

These facts alone, are sufficient to establish our claim to this country, as legitimate as that of those who fill the highest stations, by the suffrage of the people.

In no period since the existence of the ancient enlightened nations of Africa, have the prospects of the black race been brighter than

---

1 *planting States* I.e., the South, where plantations reliant upon the labor of enslaved people were an important part of the economy.
2 *husbandman* Farmer.

now; and at no time during the Christian era, have there been greater advantages presented for the advancement of any people, than at present, those which offer to the black race, both in the Eastern and Western hemispheres—our election[1] being in the Western.

Despite the efforts to the contrary, in the strenuous endeavors for a supremacy of race, the sympathies of the world in their upward tendency, are in favor of the African and black races of the earth. To be available, *we* must take advantage of these favorable feelings, and strike out for ourselves a bold and manly course, of *independent action* and *position*; otherwise, this pure and uncorrupted sympathy will be reduced to pity and contempt.

Of the countries of our choice, we have stated that one province and two islands were slaveholding places. These, as before named, are Brazil, in South America, and Cuba and Porto Rico in the West Indies. There are a few other little islands of minor consideration—the Danish, three—Swedish, one—and Dutch, four.

But in the eight last referred to, slavery is of such a mild type, that—however objectionable as such—it is merely nominal.

In South America and the Antilles, in its worst form, slavery is a blessing almost, compared with the miserable degradation of the slave under our upstart, assumed superiors, the slave-holders of the United States.

In Brazil, color is no badge of condition, and every freeman, whatever his color, is socially and politically equal, there being black gentlemen of pure African descent, filling the highest positions in State, under the Emperor. There is also an established law by the Congress of Brazil, making the crime punishable with death, for the commander of any vessel to bring into the country any human being as a slave.[2]

The following law has passed one branch of the General Legislative Assembly of Brazil, but little doubt being entertained that it will find a like favor in the other branch of that august general legislative body:

1.
All children born after the date of this law shall be free.

---

1   *election*   Choice; i.e., chosen area of focus.
2   *established law ... as a slave*   Referring to the Queirós Law of 1850, which abolished the slave trade (but not slavery itself) in Brazil.

2.

All those shall be considered free who are born in other countries, and come to Brazil after this date.

3.

Every one who serves from birth to 7 years of age, any of those included in article 1, or who has to serve so many years, at the end of 14 years shall be emancipated, and live as he chooses.

4.

Every slave paying for his liberty a sum equal to what he cost his master, or who shall gain it by honorable gratuitous title, the master shall be obliged to give him a free paper, under the penalty of article 179 of the criminal code.

5.

Where there is no stipulated price or fixed value of the slave, it shall be determined by arbitrators, one of which shall be the public *promotor*[1] of the town.

6.

The government is authorised to give precise regulations for the execution of this law, and also to form establishments necessary for taking care of those who, born after this date, may be abandoned by the owners of slaves.

7.

Opposing laws and regulations are repealed.

Concerning Cuba, there is an old established law, giving any slave the right of a certain *legal tender*, which, if refused by the slave holder, he, by going to the residence of any parish priest and making known the facts, shall immediately be declared a freeman, the priest or bishop of the parish or diocese giving him his "freedom papers." The legal tender, or sum fixed by law, we think does not exceed two hundred and fifty Spanish dollars. It may be more.

---

1 *promotor* Prosecutor.

Until the Americans intruded themselves into Cuba, contaminating society wherever they located, black and colored gentlemen and ladies of rank, mingled indiscriminately in society. But since the advent of these negro-haters, the colored people of Cuba have been reduced nearly, if not quite, to the level of the miserable degraded position of the colored people of the United States, who almost consider it a compliment and favor to receive the notice or smiles of a white.

Can we be satisfied, in this enlightened age of the world—amid the advantages which now present themselves to us—with the degradation and servility inherited from our fathers in this country? God forbid. And we think the universal reply will be—We will not.

A half century brings about a mighty change, in the reality of existing things, and events of the world's history. Fifty years ago, our fathers lived: for the most part they were sorely oppressed, debased, ignorant and incapable of comprehending the political relations of mankind; the great machinery and motive power by which the enlightened nations of the earth were impelled forward. They knew but little, and ventured to do nothing to enhance their own interests, beyond that which their oppressors taught them. They lived amidst a continual cloud of moral obscurity—a fog of bewilderment and delusion, by which they were of necessity compelled to confine themselves to a limited space—a *known* locality—lest by one step beyond this, they might have stumbled over a precipice, ruining themselves beyond recovery in the fall.

We are their sons, but not the same individuals; neither do we live in the same period with them. That which suited them, does not suit us; and that with which they may have been contented, will not satisfy us.

Without education, they were ignorant of the world and fearful of adventure. With education, we are conversant with its geography, history and nations, and delight in its enterprises and responsibilities. They once were held as slaves; to such a condition we never could be reduced. They were content with privileges; we will be satisfied with nothing less than rights. They felt themselves happy to be permitted to beg for rights; we demand them as an innate inheritance. They considered themselves favored to live by sufferance; we reject it as a degradation. A secondary position was all they asked for; we claim entire equality or nothing. The relation of master and slave was innocently acknowledged by them; we deny the right, as such, and pronounce the relation as the basest injustice that ever scourged the earth and cursed the human family. They admitted themselves to be inferiors; we barely acknowledge the whites as equals—perhaps not in every particular. They lamented their irrecoverable fate, and incapacity to redeem themselves and their race. We rejoice, that as their sons, it is our happy lot and high mission, to accomplish that which they desired and would have done, but failed for the want of ability to do.

Let no intelligent man or woman, then, among us, be found at the present day, exulting in the degradation that our enslaved parents would gladly have rid themselves, had they have had the intelligence and qualifications to accomplish their designs. Let none be found to shield themselves behind the plea of our brother bondmen in ignorance; that we know not *what* to do, nor *where* to go. We are no longer slaves, as were our fathers, but freemen; fully qualified to meet our oppressors in every relation which belongs to the elevation of man, the establishment, sustenance and perpetuity of a nation. And such a position, by the help of God our common Father, we are determined to take and maintain.

There is but one question presents itself for our serious consideration, upon which we *must* give a decisive reply—Will we transmit, as an inheritance to our children, the blessings of unrestricted civil liberty, or shall we entail upon them, as our only political legacy, the degradation and oppression left us by our fathers?

Shall we be persuaded that we can live and prosper nowhere but under the authority and power of our North American white oppressors; that this (the United States) is the country most—if not the only one—favorable to our improvement and progress? Are we willing to admit that we are incapable of self-government, establishing for ourselves such political privileges, and making such internal improvements as we delight to enjoy, after American white men have made them for themselves?

No! Neither is it true that the United States is the country best adapted to *our* improvement. But that country is the best in which our manhood—morally, mentally and physically—can be *best developed*—in which we have an untrammeled right to the enjoyment of civil and religious liberty; and the West Indies, Central and South

America, present now such advantages, superiorly preferable to all other countries.

That the continent of America was designed by Providence a reserved asylum for the various oppressed people of the earth, of all races, to us seems very apparent.

From the earliest period after the discovery, various nations sent a representative here, either as adventurers and speculators, or employed laborers, seamen, or soldiers, hired to work for their employers. And among the earliest and most numerous class who found their way to the new world, were those of the African race. And it has been ascertained to our minds beyond a doubt, that when the Continent was discovered, there were found in the West Indies and Central America, tribes of the black race, fine looking people, having the usual characteristics of color and hair, identifying them as being originally of the African race; no doubt, being a remnant of the Africans who, with the Carthaginian expedition, were adventitiously cast upon this continent, in their memorable adventure to the "Great Island," after sailing many miles distant to the West of the "Pillars of Hercules"[1]—the present Straits of Gibraltar.

We would not be thought to be superstitious, when we say, that in all this we can "see the finger of God."[2] Is it not worthy of a notice here, that while the ingress of foreign whites to this continent has been voluntary and constant, and that of the blacks involuntary and but occasional, yet the whites in the southern part have *decreased* in numbers, *degenerated* in character, and become mentally and physically *enervated* and imbecile; while the blacks and colored people have studiously *increased* in numbers, *regenerated* in character, and have grown mentally and physically vigorous and active, developing every

---

1 *Pillars of Hercules* Two masses of land that border the Strait of Gibraltar, which links the Mediterranean Sea and the Atlantic Ocean. In positing that ancient Africans (Carthaginians) may have explored as far as the Americas (the "Great Island"), Delany may be alluding to comments made by some ancient Greek writers; Plato's Timaeus, for example, imagines a past empire of Atlantis extending from Egypt to a "great Island" located beyond the "Pillars of Hercules," while Herodotus suggests that in the first millennium BCE the Phoenicians (whose empire included Carthage and other parts of northern Africa) traveled extensively beyond the Pillars.

2 *finger of God* Phrase used numerous times in the Bible, in reference especially to the inscription of the tablets bearing the Ten Commandments; it is also used in reference to the punishments God inflicts on the Egyptians for the Pharaoh's refusal to release the Israelites from slavery. See, for example, Exodus 8.19 and 31.18.

function of their manhood, and are now, in their elementary character, decidedly superior to the white race? So then the white race could never successfully occupy the southern portion of the continent; they must of necessity, every generation, be repeopled from another quarter of the globe. The fatal error committed by the Spaniards, under Pizarro,[1] was the attempt to exterminate the Incas and Peruvians, and fill their places by European whites. The Peruvian Indians, a hale, hardy, vigorous, intellectual race of people, were succeeded by those who soon became idle, vicious, degenerated and imbecile. But Peru, like all the other South American States, is regaining her former potency, just in proportion as the European race decreases among them. All the labor of the country is performed by the aboriginal natives and the blacks; the few Europeans there, being the merest excrescences on the body politic—consuming drones in the social hive.

Had we no other claims than those set forth in a foregoing part of this Address, they are sufficient to induce every black and colored person to remain on this continent, unshaken and unmoved.

But the West Indians, Central and South Americans, are a noble race of people; generous, sociable and tractable—just the people with whom we desire to unite, who are susceptible of progress, improvement and reform of every kind. They now desire all the improvements of North America, but being justly jealous of their rights, they have no confidence in the whites of the United States, and consequently peremptorily refuse to permit an indiscriminate settlement among them of this class of people; but placing every confidence in the black and colored people of North America.

The example of the unjust invasion and forcible seizure of a large portion of the territory of Mexico,[2] is still fresh in their memory; and the oppressive disfranchisement of a large number of native Mexicans, by the Americans—because of the color and race of the natives—will continue to rankle in the bosom of the people of those countries,

---

1 *Pizarro* Francisco Pizarro (c. 1471–1541), Spanish explorer who led the expedition to Peru that resulted in the conquest of the Inca Empire.

2 *unjust invasion ... of Mexico* Referring to the 1845 American annexation of Texas (part of Mexico until 1836) and the ensuing Mexican–American War (1846–48). The United States seized territories in which the Indigenous people had been Mexican citizens, but did not allow them American citizenship until the twentieth century.

and prove a sufficient barrier henceforth against the inroads of North American whites among them.

Upon the American continent, then, we are determined to remain, despite every opposition that may be urged against us.

You will doubtless be asked—and that, too, with an air of seriousness—why, if desirable to remain on this continent, not be content to remain *in* the United States. The objections to this—and potent reasons, too, in our estimation—have already been clearly shown.

But notwithstanding all this, were there still any rational, nay, even the most futile grounds for hope, we still might be stupid enough to be content to remain, and yet through another period of unexampled patience and suffering, continue meekly to drag the galling yoke and clank the chain of servility and degradation. But whether or not in this, God is to be thanked and Heaven blessed, we are not permitted, despite our willingness and stupidity, to indulge even the most distant glimmer of a hope of attaining to the level of a well protected slave.

For years, we have been studiously and jealously observing the course of political events and policy, on the part of this country, both in a national and individual State capacity, as pursued towards the colored people. And he who, in the midst of them, can live without observation, is either excusably ignorant, or reprehensibly deceptious and untrustworthy.

We deem it entirely unnecessary to tax you with anything like the history of even one chapter of the unequalled infamies perpetrated on the part of the various States, and national decrees, by legislation, against us. But we shall call your particular attention to the more recent acts of the United States; because whatever privileges we may enjoy in any individual State, will avail nothing, when not recognized as such by the United States.

When the condition of the inhabitants of any country is fixed by legal grades of distinction, this condition can never be changed except by express legislation. And it is the height of folly to expect such express legislation, except by the inevitable force of some irresistible internal political pressure. The force necessary to this imperative demand on our part, we never can obtain, because of our numerical feebleness.

Were the interests of the common people identical with ours, we, in this, might succeed, because we, as a class, would then be numerically the superior. But this is not a question of the rich against the poor, nor the common people against the higher classes; but a question of white against black—every white person, by legal right, being held superior to a black or colored person.

In Russia, the common people might obtain an equality with the aristocracy; because, of the sixty-five millions of her population, forty-five millions are serfs or peasants—leaving but twenty millions of the higher classes, royalty, nobility and all included.

The rights of no oppressed people have ever yet been obtained by a voluntary act of justice on the part of the oppressors. Christians, philanthropists, and moralists may preach, argue and philosophise as they may to the contrary; facts are against them. Voluntary acts, it is true, which are in themselves just, may sometimes take place on the part of the oppressor; but these are always actuated by the force of some outward circumstances of self-interest, equal to a compulsion.

The boasted liberties of the American people were established by a Constitution, borrowed from and modeled after the British *magna carta*.[1] And this great charter of British liberty, so much boasted of and vaunted as a model bill of rights, was obtained only by force and extortion.

The Barons, an order of noblemen, under the reign of King John, becoming dissatisfied at the terms submitted to by their sovereign, which necessarily brought degradation upon themselves—terms prescribed by the insolent Pope Innocent III, the haughty sovereign Pontiff of Rome—summoned his majesty to meet them on the plains of the memorable meadow of Runnimede,[2] where, presenting to him their own Bill of Rights—a bill dictated by themselves, and drawn up by their own hands—at the unsheathed points of a thousand glittering swords, they commanded him, against his will, to sign the extraordinary document. There was no alternative; he must either do or die. With puerile timidity, he leaned forward his rather commanding but imbecile person, and with a trembling hand and single dash of the pen, the name KING JOHN stood forth in bold relief, sending more

---

1   *magna carta*   English charter of rights signed by King John in 1215, setting out limits on the exercise of power by the monarch. The charter, which originated in a conflict between the monarchy and various rebel factions, has long been a symbol of formally enshrined political freedoms.

2   *Runnimede*   Meadow along the River Thames, west of central London.

terror throughout the world, than the mystic hand-writing of Heaven throughout the dominions of Nebuchadnezzar, blazing on the walls of Babylon.[1] A consternation, not because of the *name* of the King, but because of the rights of *others*, which that name acknowledged.

The King, however, soon became dissatisfied, and determining on a revocation of the act—an act done entirely contrary to his will—at the head of a formidable army, spread fire and sword throughout the kingdom.

But the Barons, though compelled to leave their castles—their houses and homes—and fly for their lives, could not be induced to undo that which they had so nobly done; the achievement of their rights and privileges. Hence, the act has stood throughout all suc-ceeding time, because never annulled by those who *willed* it.

It will be seen that the first great modern Bill of Rights was obtained only by a force of arms: a resistance of the people against the injus-tice and intolerance of their rulers. We say the people—because that which the Barons demanded for themselves, was afterwards extended to the common people. Their only hope was based on their *superiority of numbers.*

But can we in this country hope for as much? Certainly not. Our case is a hopeless one. There was but *one* John, with his few sprigs of adhering royalty; and but *one* heart at which the threatening points of their swords were directed by a thousand Barons; while in our case, there is but a handful of the oppressed, without a sword to point, and *twenty millions* of Johns or Jonathans[2]—as you please—with as many hearts, tenfold more relentless than that of Prince John Lackland,[3] and as deceptive and hypocritical as the Italian heart of Innocent III.

Where, then, is our hope of success in this country? Upon what is it based? Upon what principle of political policy and sagacious discern-ment, do our political leaders and acknowledged great men—colored men we mean—justify themselves by telling us, and insisting that

---

1   *Nebuchadnezzar ... Babylon*   See Daniel 5, in which mystical handwriting appears on the wall in the hall of King Belshazzar, son of Nebuchadnezzar, telling him that his days as king are numbered because he has not honored God. Belshazzar is terrified by the ghostly writing and slain later that night.

2   *Jonathans*   "Jonathan" or "Brother Jonathan" was a generic epithet for Americans, espe-cially those from New England.

3   *Prince John Lackland*   Nickname for King John of England.

we shall believe them, and submit to what they say—to be patient, remain where we are; that there is a "bright prospect and glorious future" before us in this country! May Heaven open our eyes from their Bartemian[1] obscurity.

But we call your attention to another point of our political degradation. The acts of State and general governments.

In a few of the States, as in New York, the colored inhabitants have a partial privilege of voting a white man into office. This privilege is based on a property qualification of two hundred and fifty dollars worth of real estate. In others, as in Ohio, in the absence of organic provision, the privilege is granted by judicial decision, based on a ratio of blood, of an admixture of more than one-half white; while in many of the States, there is no privilege allowed, either partial or unrestricted.

The policy of the above-named States will be seen and detected at a glance, which while seeming to extend immunities, is intended especially for the object of degradation.

In the State of New York, for instance, there is a constitutional distinction created among colored men—almost necessarily compelling one part to feel superior to the other; while among the whites no such distinctions dare be known. Also, in Ohio, there is a legal distinction set up by an upstart judiciary, creating among the colored people, a privileged class by birth! All this must necessarily sever the cords of union among us, creating almost insurmountable prejudices of the most stupid and fatal kind, paralysing the last bracing nerve which promised to give us strength.

It is upon this same principle, and for the selfsame object, that the General Government has long been endeavoring, and is at present knowingly designing to effect a recognition of the independence of the Dominican Republic, while disparagingly refusing to recognize the independence of the Haitian nation[2]—a people four-fold greater in numbers, wealth and power. The Haitians, it is pretended, are refused because they are *Negroes*; while the Dominicans, as is well known to all who are familiar with the geography, history, and political relations of that people, are identical—except in language, they

---

1   *Bartemian*   Alluding to Bartimaeus, a blind man healed by Jesus in Mark 10.46–52.
2   *General Government ... Haitian nation*   The United States government refused to recognize Haiti's independence until 1862.

speaking the Spanish tongue—with those of the Haitians; being composed of negroes and a mixed race. The government may shield itself by the plea that it is not familiar with the origin of those people. To this we have but to reply, that if the government is thus ignorant of the relations of its near neighbors, it is the height of presumption, and no small degree of assurance, for it to set up itself as capable of prescribing terms to the one, or conditions to the other.

Should they accomplish their object, they then will have succeeded in forever establishing a barrier of impassable separation, by the creation of a political distinction between those people, of superiority and inferiority of origin or national existence. Here, then, is another stratagem of this most determined and untiring enemy of our race—the government of the United States.

We come now to the crowning act of infamy on the part of the General Government towards the colored inhabitants of the United States—an act so vile in its nature, that rebellion against its demands should be promptly made, in every attempt to enforce its infernal provisions.

In the history of national existence, there is not to be found a parallel to the tantalising insult and aggravating despotism of the provisions of Millard Fillmore's Fugitive Slave Bill,[1] passed by the thirty-third Congress of the United States, with the approbation of a majority of the American people, in the year of the Gospel of Jesus Christ, eighteen hundred and fifty.

This Bill had but one object in its provisions, which was fully accomplished in its passage; that is, the reduction of every colored person in the United States—save those who carry free papers of emancipation, or bills of sale from former claimants or owners—to a state of relative *slavery*; placing each and every one of us at the *disposal of any and every white* who might choose to *claim* us, and the caprice of any and every upstart knave bearing the title of "Commissioner."

Did any of you, fellow-countrymen, reside in a country the pro-

---

1   *Millard Fillmore's Fugitive Slave Bill*   One of the most controversial political decisions of the pre-Civil War era, the Fugitive Slave Act of 1850 was enacted as a "compromise" between free and slave states; it criminalized any aiding of persons escaping slavery, and vastly increased the risk to free African Americans, North and South, of being falsely claimed as a slaveowner's property. Millard Fillmore served as president from 1850 to 1853, and as such played a significant role in the passing of the new legislation.

visions of whose laws were such that any person of a certain class, who, whenever he, she or they pleased, might come forward, lay a claim to, make oath before (it might be), some stupid and heartless person, authorized to decide in such cases, and take, at their option, your horse, cow, sheep, house and lot, or any other property, bought and paid for by your own earnings—the result of your personal toil and labor—would you be willing, or could you be induced, by any reasoning, however great the source from which it came, to remain in that country? We pause, fellow-countrymen, for a reply.

If there be not one yea, of how much more importance, then, is your *own personal safety*, than that of property? Of how much more concern is the safety of a wife or husband, than that of a cow or horse; a child, than a sheep; the destiny of your family, to that of a house and lot?

And yet this is precisely our condition. Any one of us, at any moment, is liable to be *claimed*, *seized* and *taken* into custody by any white, as his or her property—to be *enslaved for life*—and there is no remedy, because it is the *law of the land*! And we dare predict, and take this favorable opportunity to forewarn you, fellow-countrymen, that the time is not far distant, when there will be carried on by the white men of this nation, an extensive commerce in the persons of what now compose the free colored people of the North. We forewarn you, that the general enslavement of the whole of this class of people, is now being contemplated by the whites.

At present, we are liable to enslavement at any moment, provided we are taken *away* from our homes. But we dare venture further to forewarn you, that the scheme is in mature contemplation, and has even been mooted in high places, of harmonizing the two discordant political divisions in the country, by again reducing the free to slave States.

The completion of this atrocious scheme, only becomes necessary for each and every one of us to find an owner and master at our own doors. Let the general government but pass such a law, and the States will comply as an act of harmony. Let the South but *demand* it, and the North will comply as a *duty* of compromise.

If Pennsylvania, New York and Massachusetts can be found arming their sons as watch-dogs for southern slave hunters; if the United States may, with impunity, garrison with troops the Court House of the freest city in America; blockade the streets; station armed ruffians of dragoons, and spiked artillery in hostile awe of the people; if free, white, high-born and bred gentlemen of Boston and New York, are smitten down to the earth,[1] refused an entrance on professional business, into the Court Houses, until inspected by a slave hunter and his counsel; all to put down the liberty of the black man; then, indeed, is there no hope for us in this country!

It is, fellow-countrymen, a fixed fact, as indelible as the Covenant of God in the Heavens, that the colored people of these United States, are the slaves of any white person who may choose to claim them!

What safety or guarantee have we for ourselves or families? Let us, for a moment, examine this point.

Supposing some hired spy of the slave power, residing in Illinois, whom, for illustration, we shall call Stephen A., Counsel B., a mercenary hireling of New York, and Commissioner C., a slave-catcher of Pennsylvania, should take umbrage at the acts or doings of any colored person or persons in a free State; they may with impunity, send or go on their knight errands to the South, (as did a hireling of the slave power in New York—a lawyer by profession), give a description of such person or persons, and an agent with warrants may be immediately despatched to swear them into slavery forever.

We tell you, fellow-countrymen, any one of you here assembled— your humble committee who report to you this address—may, by the laws of this land, be seized, whatever the circumstances of his birth; whether he descends from free or slave parents—whether born North or South of Mason and Dixon's Line[2]—and ere the setting of

---

1   [Delany's note]   John Jay, Esq., of New York, son of the late distinguished jurist, Hon. Wm. Jay, was, in 1852, as the counsel of a Fugitive Slave, brutally assaulted and struck in the face by the slave catching agent and counsel, Busteed. Also, Mr. Dana, an honorable gentleman, counsel for the fugitive Burns, one of the first literary men of Boston, was arrested on his entrance into the Court House, and not permitted to pass the guard of slave-catchers, till the slave agent and counsel, Loring, together with the overseer, Suttle, *inspected* him, and ordered that he might be *allowed* to pass in! After which, in passing along the street, Mr. Dana was ruffianly assaulted and murderously felled to the earth, by the minions of the dastardly Southern overseer.

2   *Mason and Dixon's Line*   Drawn in the 1760s by English surveyors Charles Mason and Jeremiah Dixon, the Mason-Dixon line originally formed the border between Pennsylvania and Maryland; over the coming century it came to signify the border between the American North and South, and thereby the literal and symbolic border between the free states and the slave states.

another sun, be speeding his way to that living sepulchre,[1] and death chamber of our race—the curse and scourge of this country—the Southern part of the United States. This is not idle speculation, but living, naked, undisguised truth.

A member of your committee has received a letter from a gentleman of respectability and standing in the South, who writes to the following effect. We copy his own words:

> There are at this moment, as I was to-day informed by Colonel W., one of our first magistrates in this city, a gang of from twenty-five to thirty vagabonds of poor white men, who for twenty-five dollars a head, clear of all expenses, are ready and willing to go to the North, make acquaintance with the blacks in various places, send their descriptions to unprincipled slave holders here—for there are many of this kind to be found among the poorer class of masters—and swear them into bondage. So the free blacks, as well as fugitive slaves, will have to keep a sharp watch over themselves to get clear of this scheme to enslave them.

Here, then, you have but a paragraph in the great volume of this political crusade, and legislative pirating by the American people, over the rights and privileges of the colored inhabitants of the country. If this be but a paragraph—for such it is in truth—what must be the contents when the whole history is divulged! Never will the contents of this dreadful record of crime, corruption and oppression be fully revealed, until the Trump[2] of God shall proclaim the universal summons to judgment. Then, and then alone, shall the whole truth be acknowledged, when the doom of the criminal shall be forever sealed.

We desire not to be sentimental, but rather would be political; and therefore call your attention to another point—a point already referred to.

In giving the statistics of various countries, and preferences to many places herein mentioned, as points of destination in emigration, we have said little or nothing concerning the present governments, the various State departments, nor the condition of society among the people.

---

1   *sepulchre* Tomb or burial-place.
2   *Trump* Trumpet.

This is not the province of your committee, but the legitimate office of a Board of Foreign Commissioners, whom there is no doubt will be created by the Convention, with provisions and instructions to report thereon, in due season, of their mission.

With a few additional remarks on the subject of the British Provinces of North America, we shall have done our duty, and completed, for the time being, the arduous, important and momentous task assigned to us.

The British Provinces of North America, especially Canada West—formerly called Upper Canada—in climate, soil, productions, and the usual prospects for internal improvements, are equal, if not superior, to any northern part of the continent. And for these very reasons, aside from their contiguity to the northern part of the United States—and consequent facility for the escape of the slaves from the South—we certainly should prefer them as a place of destination. We love the Canadas, and admire their laws, because as British Provinces, there is no difference known among the people—no distinction of race. And we deem it a duty to recommend that, for the present, as a temporary asylum, it is certainly advisable for every colored person, who desiring to emigrate, and is not prepared for any other destination, to locate in Canada West.

Every advantage on our part, should be now taken of the opportunity of *obtaining* LANDS, while they are to be had cheap and on the most easy conditions, from the Government.

Even those who never contemplate a removal from this country of chains, it will be their best interest and greatest advantage, to procure lands in the Canadian Provinces. It will be an easy, profitable and safe investment, even should they never occupy nor yet see them. We shall then be but doing what the whites in the United States have for years been engaged in; securing unsettled lands in the territories, previous to their enhancement in value, by the force of settlement and progressive neighboring improvements. There are also at present, great openings for colored people to enter into the various industrial departments of business operations: laborers, mechanics, teachers, merchants and shop-keepers, and professional men of every kind. These places are now open, as much to the colored as the white man, in Canada, with little or no opposition to his progress; at least in the character of prejudicial preferences on account of race. And all of these, without any hesitancy, do we most cheerfully recommend to the colored inhabitants of the United States.

But our preference to other places, over the Canadas, has been cursorily stated in the foregoing part of this paper; and since the writing of that part, it would seem that the predictions or apprehensions concerning the Provinces, are about to be verified by the British Parliament and Home Government themselves. They have virtually conceded, and openly expressed it—Lord Brougham in the lead—that the English Provinces of North America must, ere long, cease to be a part of the British domain, and become annexed to the United States.[1]

It is needless—however much we may regret the necessity of its acknowledgment—for us to stop our ears, shut our eyes, and stultify our senses against the truth in this matter; since by so doing, it does not alter the case. Every political movement, both in England and the United States, favors such an issue, and the sooner we acknowledge it, the better it will be for our cause, ourselves individually, and the destiny of our people in this country.

These Provinces have long been burdensome to the British nation, and her statesmen have long since discovered and decided as an indisputable predicate in political economy, that any province as an independent State, is more profitable in a commercial consideration to a country, than when depending as one of its colonies. As a child to the parent, or an apprentice to his master, so is a colony to a State. And as the man who enters into business is to the manufacturer and importer, so is the colony which becomes an independent State, to the country from which it recedes.

Great Britain is decidedly a commercial and money-making nation, and counts closely on her commercial relations with any country. That nation or people which puts the largest amount of money into her coffers, are the people who may expect to obtain her

---

1   *They have virtually ... United States* Though the War of 1812 had been the last explicit attempt by the U.S. to conquer what were then the British provinces of Upper and Lower Canada, small-scale movements in favor of annexing Canada to the United States continued to emerge throughout the nineteenth century, often linked to the American ideals of westward expansion. On the American side, some annexationists were in favor of extending proslavery interests; many others in both Canada and America supported annexation for other economic and political reasons. The abolitionist Brougham was Lord Chancellor of Great Britain from 1830 to 1834.

greatest favors. This the Americans do; consequently—and we candidly ask you to mark the prediction—the British will interpose little or no obstructions to the Canadas, Cuba, or any other province or colony contiguous to this country, falling into the American Union; except only in such cases where there would be a compromise of her honor. And in the event of a seizure of any of these, there would be no necessity for such a sacrifice; it could readily be avoided by diplomacy.

Then, there is little hope for us on this continent, short of those places where by reason of their numbers, there is the greatest combination of strength and interests on the part of the colored race.

We have ventured to predict a reduction of the now nominally free into slave States. Already has this "reign of terror" and dreadful work of destruction commenced. We give you the quotation from a Mississippi paper, which will readily be admitted as authority in this case:

> Two years ago a law was passed by the California Legislature granting *one year* to the owners of slaves carried into the territory previous to the adoption of the Constitution, to remove them beyond the limits of the State. Last year the provision of this law *was extended twelve months longer*. We learn by the late California papers that a bill has just passed the Assembly, by a vote of 33 to 21, *continuing the same law in force until* 1855. The provisions of this bill embraces *slaves who have been carried to California since the adoption of her Constitution*, as well as those who were there previously. The large majority by which it passed, and the opinions advanced during the discussion, *indicates a more favorable state of sentiment in regard to the rights of slave holders in California than we supposed existed.*—(*Mississippian*)

No one who is a general and intelligent observer of the politics of this country, will, after reading this, doubt for a moment the final result.

At present, there is a proposition under consideration in California, to authorize the holding of a Convention to amend the Constitution of that State, which doubtless will be carried into effect; when there is no doubt that a clause will be inserted, granting the right to *hold slaves at discretion* in the State.[1] This being done, it will meet with general

---

1 *At present ... in the State* Although California did ultimately remain a free state leading up to the Civil War, proslavery factions there gained strength throughout the 1850s, and the state enacted its own harsh Fugitive Slave Law in 1852.

favor throughout the country by the American people, and the *policy be adopted on the State's right principle.*[1] This alone is necessary, in addition to the insufferable Fugitive Slave Law, and the recent nefarious Nebraska Bill[2]—which is based upon this very boasted American policy of the State's right principle—to reduce the free to slave States, without a murmur from the people. And did not the Nebraska Bill disrespect the feelings and infringe upon the political rights of Northern *white* people, its adoption would be hailed with loud shouts of approbation, from Portland to San Francisco.

That, then, which is left for us to do, is to *secure* our liberty; a position which shall fully *warrant* us *against* the *liability* of such monstrous political crusades and riotous invasions of our rights. Nothing less than a national indemnity, indelibly fixed by virtue of our own sovereign potency, will satisfy us as a redress of grievances for the unparalleled wrongs, undisguised impositions, and unmitigated oppression, which we have suffered at the hands of this American people.

And what wise politician would otherwise conclude and determine? None, we dare say. And a people who are incapable of this discernment and precaution, are incapable of self-government, and incompetent to direct their own political destiny. For our own part, we spurn to treat for liberty on any other terms or conditions.

It may not be inapplicable, in this particular place, to quote from high authority, language which has fallen under our notice, since this report has been under our consideration. The quotation is worth nothing, except to show that the position assumed by us, is a natural one, which constitutes the essential basis of self-protection.

Said Earl Aberdeen recently in the British House of Lords, when referring to the great question which is now agitating Europe:[3] "One

---

1   *State's right principle*   I.e., the power of individual states to overrule federal laws, a power states possessed in much higher degree prior to the Civil War. California had been admitted into the Union as a free state as part of the Compromise of 1850.

2   *Nebraska Bill*   The Kansas-Nebraska Act of 1854, which created the territories of Kansas and Nebraska, left the question of slavery's legality up to the popular sovereignty of future states on this land. This was in direct violation of the 1821 Missouri Compromise, which held that land north of the 36°30′ parallel would be free of slavery.

3   *the great question ... Europe*   Delany refers to the Crimean War, which Britain had entered in 1854, allying with the French Empire and the Ottoman Empire against [continued ...]

thing alone is certain, that the only way to obtain a sure and honorable peace, is to *acquire a position* which may *command* it; and to gain such a position *every nerve and sinew* of the empire should be strained. The pickpocket who robs us is not to be let off because he offers to restore our purse"; and his Grace might have justly added, "should never thereafter be intrusted or confided in."

The plea doubtless will be, as it already frequently has been raised, that to remove from the United States, our slave brethren would be left without a hope. They already find their way in large companies to the Canadas, and they have only to be made sensible that there is as much freedom for them South, as there is North; as much protection in Mexico as in Canada; and the fugitive slave will find it a much pleasanter journey and more easy of access, to wend his way from Louisiana and Arkansas to Mexico, than thousands of miles through the slave-holders of the South and slave-catchers of the North, to Canada. Once into Mexico, and his farther exit to Central and South America and the West Indies, would be certain. There would be no obstructions whatever. No miserable, half-starved, servile Northern slave-catchers by the way, waiting cap in hand, ready and willing to do the bidding of their contemptible southern masters.

No prisons, nor Court Houses, as slave-pens and garrisons, to secure the fugitive and rendezvous the mercenary gangs, who are bought as military on such occasions. No perjured Marshals, bribed Commissioners, nor hireling counsel, who, spaniel-like, crouch at the feet of Southern slave-holders, and cringingly tremble at the crack of their whip. No, not as may be encountered throughout his northern flight, there are none of these to be found or met with in his travels from the Bravo del Norte to the dashing Oronoco[1]—from the borders of Texas to the boundaries of Peru.

Should anything occur to prevent a successful emigration to the South—Central, South America, and the West Indies—we have no hesitancy, rather than remain in the United States, the merest subordinates and serviles of the whites, should the Canadas still continue

---

the Russian Empire. George Hamilton-Gordon, 4th Earl of Aberdeen, served as British prime minister for the duration of the war.

1 *Bravo del Norte* Also known as the Rio Grande, a river that flows from the southern United States to northern Mexico; *Oronoco* Among the longest rivers in South America, flowing from Venezuela to Colombia.

separate in their political relations from this country, to recommend to the great body of our people, to remove to Canada West, where being politically equal to the whites, physically united with each other by a concentration of strength; when worse comes to worse, we may be found, not as a scattered, weak and impotent people, as we now are separated from each other throughout the Union, but a united and powerful body of freemen, mighty in politics, and terrible in any conflict which might ensue, in the event of an attempt at the disturbance of our political relations, domestic repose, and peaceful firesides.

Now, fellow-countrymen, we have done. Into your ears have we recounted your own sorrows; before your own eyes have we exhibited your wrongs; into your own hands have we committed your own cause. If these should prove a failure to remedy this dreadful evil, to assuage this terrible curse which has come upon us, the fault will be yours and not ours, since we have offered you a healing balm for every sorely aggravated wound.

—1854

from *Blake; or, the Huts of America*

Delany's only novel, *Blake*, made little impact upon its serialized publication between 1859 and 1862, but it is today acknowledged by many critics as one of the most important and remarkable American novels of the nineteenth century. The work tells of Henry Holland (later known by the name Henry Blake), who flees slavery and endeavors to instigate a mass rebellion of the enslaved after the sudden sale of his wife, Maggie, to a Northerner who plans to keep Maggie in slavery at her winter residence in Cuba. Over time, it is revealed that Henry was born free as "Henrico Blacus" in the West Indies, but was kidnapped and sold into slavery as a young man; Henry's sense of freedom as his birthright becomes a significant aspect of his leadership as he spreads the word of revolution, first throughout the southern United States, and later in Cuba.

Set roughly in the years 1852 to 1853, *Blake*, which regularly alludes to real-world people and events, is considered by some modern critics to be an early experiment with the genre of alternative history. The revolution promised in the novel's early chapters, however, never occurs; the final chapters of Part Two were likely published in the May 1862 issues of *The Weekly Anglo-African*, but those issues of the magazine have since been lost, and no manuscript copy of the text is extant. The work virtually disappeared from public consciousness until the mid-twentieth century; nevertheless, *Blake's* radical interpretation of Christianity, and its insistence that open resistance and even violence were appropriate means of achieving black liberation, make the novel itself revolutionary.

Chapter 1
The Project

On one of those exciting occasions, during a contest for the Presidency of the United States,[1] a number of gentlemen met in the city of Baltimore. They were few in number, and appeared little concerned about the affairs of the general government. Though men of intelligence, their time and attention appeared to be entirely absorbed

---

1   *a contest ... United States* The presidential election of 1852, which saw the Democrat Franklin Pierce elected to the presidency; though he was a Northerner who claimed to be morally opposed to slavery, Pierce did nothing to pursue abolition and in fact encouraged legislation that allowed the westward expansion of slavery. Pierce's main opponent was the Whig Winfield Scott, with a third party, the antislavery Free Soil Party, gaining approximately 5 per cent of the popular vote.

in an adventure of self interest. They met for the purpose of completing arrangements for refitting the old ship *Merchantman*, which then lay in the harbor near Fells Point. Colonel Stephen Franks, Major James Armsted, Captain Richard Paul and Captain George Royer, composed those who represented the American side—Captain Juan Garcia and Captain Jose Castello, those of Cuban interest.[1]

Here a conversation ensued upon what seemed a point of vital importance to the company; it related to the place best suited for the completion of their arrangements. The Americans insisted on Baltimore as affording the greatest facilities, and having done more for the encouragement and protection of the trade than any other known place. Whilst the Cubans, on the other side, urged their objections on the ground that the continual increase of liberal principles in the various political parties, which were fast ushering into existence, made the objection beyond a controversy. Havana was contended for as a point best suited for adjusting their arrangements, and that too with many apparent reasons; but for some cause, the preference for Baltimore prevailed.

Subsequently to the adjustment of their affairs by the most complete arrangement for refitting the vessel, Col. Franks took leave of the party for his home in the distant State of Mississippi.

CHAPTER 2
COLONEL FRANKS AT HOME

On the return of Col. Stephen Franks to his home at Natchez,[2] he met there Mrs. Arabella, the wife of Judge Ballard, an eminent jurist of one of the Northern states. She had arrived but a day before him, on a visit to some relatives, of whom Mrs. Franks was one. The

---

1   *an adventure ... Cuban interest*   The implication in this opening paragraph is that the men are gathering to strike a deal concerning the trade of enslaved people, using the *Merchantman* to illegally transport their human cargo. While the U.S. had ended its participation in the international slave trade in 1808, with the Act Prohibiting Importation of Slaves, such illicit transactions remained relatively commonplace due to the continued legality of both slavery and the international slave trade in Spanish-controlled Cuba (slavery there was not formally abolished until 1886). Many proslavery Americans in the 1840s and 1850s were in favor of annexing Cuba as a slave state, a movement that Franklin Pierce openly supported.
2   *Natchez*   City in Mississippi, notable for its many cotton plantations.

conversation, as is customary on the meeting of Americans residing in such distant latitudes, readily turned on the general policy of the country.

Mrs. Ballard possessed the highest intelligence, and Mrs. Maria Franks was among the most accomplished of Southern ladies.

"Tell me, Madam Ballard, how will the North go in the present issue?"[1] enquired Franks.

"Give yourself no concern about that, Colonel," replied Mrs. Ballard, "you will find the North true to the country."

"What you consider true, may be false—that is, it might be true to you, and false to us," continued he.

"You do not understand me, Colonel," she rejoined, "we can have no interests separate from yours; you know the time-honored motto, 'united we stand,' and so forth, must apply to the American people under every policy in every section of the Union."

"So it should, but amidst the general clamor in the contest for ascendency, may you not lose sight of this important point?"

"How can we? You, I'm sure, Colonel, know very well that in our country commercial interests have taken precedence of all others, which is a sufficient guarantee of our fidelity to the South."

"That may be, madam, but we are still apprehensive."

"Well sir, we certainly do not know what more to do to give you assurance of our sincerity. We have as a plight of faith yielded Boston, New York, and Philadelphia—the intelligence and wealth of the North—in carrying out the Compromise measures for the interests of the South;[2] can we do more?"

"True, Madam Ballard, true! I yield the controversy. You have already done more than we of the South expected. I now remember

---

1   *the present issue* I.e., the presidential election.

2   *We have ... the South* Mrs. Ballard refers to the Compromise of 1850, a series of acts meant to defuse the increasing divergence of political interests between the North and the South, particularly on the matter of slavery. Most significantly, the Fugitive Slave Act mandated increased efforts on the part of free states to hunt down and arrest fugitives from slavery, while also imposing fines and jail time on anyone who assisted such fugitives. The Act was highly controversial throughout the North—even among whites who did not strongly oppose slavery, but who saw the new legislation as an encroachment of the Southern slave power upon the Northern states' rights.

that the Judge himself, tried the first case under the Act, in your city, by which the measures were tested."[1]

"He did, sir, and if you will not consider me unwomanly by telling you, desired me, on coming here, to seek every opportunity to give the fullest assurance that the judiciary are sound on that question. Indeed, so far as an individual might be concerned, his interests in another direction as you know, place him beyond suspicion," concluded Mrs. Ballard.

"I am satisfied, madam, and by your permission, arrest the conversation. My acknowledgements, madam!" bowed the Colonel, with true southern courtesy.

"Maria, my dear, you look careworn; are you indisposed?" inquired Franks of his wife, who during conversation sat silent.

"Not physically, Colonel," replied she, "but—"

Just at this moment a servant throwing open the door announced dinner.

Besides a sprightly black boy of some ten years of age, there was in attendance a prepossessing, handsome maidservant, who generally kept, as much as the occasion would permit, behind the chair of her mistress. A mutual attachment appeared to exist between them, the maid apparently disinclined to leave the mistress, who seemed to keep her as near her person as possible.

Now and again the fat cook, mammy Judy, would appear at the door of the dining room bearing a fresh supply for the table, who with a slight nod of the head, accompanied with an affectionate smile and the word "Maggie," indicated a tie much closer than that of mere fellow-servants.

Maggie had long been the favorite maidservant of her mistress, having attained the position through merit. She was also nurse and foster-mother to the two last children of Mrs. Franks, and loved them, to all appearance, as her own. The children reciprocated this affection, calling her "mammy."

Mammy Judy, who for years had occupied this position, ceded it to her daughter, she preferring, in consequence of age, the less active life of the culinary department.

---

1   *tried the first case … tested* Delany alludes to cases such as that of Thomas Sims, who fled enslavement in Georgia in 1851; Sims's trial in Boston, which saw him forcibly returned to enslavement, was among the first and most famous of such trials that took place in the early 1850s.

The boy Tony would frequently cast a comic look upon Mrs. Ballard, then imploringly gaze in the face of his mistress. So intent was he in this, that twice did his master admonish him by a nod of the head.

"My dear," said the Colonel, "you are dull today; pray tell me what makes you sad?"

"I am not bodily afflicted, colonel Franks, but my spirit is heavy," she replied.

"How so? What is the matter?"

"That will best be answered at another time and place, colonel."

Giving his head an unconscious scratch accompanied with a slight twitch of the corner of the mouth, Franks seemed to comprehend the whole of it.

On one of her Northern tours to the watering places,[1] during a summer season some two years previous, having with her Maggie the favorite, Mrs. Franks visited the family of the Judge, at which time Mrs. Ballard first saw the maid. She was a dark mulatto[2] of a rich, yellow, autumn-like complexion, with a matchless, cushion-like head of hair, neither straight nor curly, but handsomer than either.

Mrs. Franks was herself a handsome lady of some thirty-five summers, but ten years less in appearance, a little above medium height, between the majestic and graceful, raven black hair, and dark, expressive eyes. Yet it often had been whispered that in beauty the maid equalled if not exceeded the mistress. Her age was twenty-eight.

The conduct of Mrs. Franks toward her servant was more like that of an elder sister than a mistress, and the mistress and maid sometimes wore dresses cut from the same web of cloth. Mrs. Franks would frequently adjust the dress and see that the hair of her maid was properly arranged. This to Mrs. Ballard was as unusual as it was an objectionable sight, especially as she imagined there was an air of hauteur in her demeanor. It was then she determined to subdue her spirit.

Acting from this impulse, several times in her absence, Mrs. Ballard took occasion to administer to the maid severities she had never

---

1   *the watering places*   Resort towns located by the sea or by natural mineral springs.

2   *mulatto*   Term used in the nineteenth century to refer to an individual of mixed racial background—typically, someone with one white parent and one parent of African descent. (It is today considered archaic and offensive.)

experienced at the hands of her mistress, giving her at one time a severe slap on the cheek, calling her an "impudent jade."[1]

At this, Mrs. Franks, on learning, was quite surprised, but on finding that the maid gave no just cause for it, took no further notice of it, designedly evading the matter. But before leaving, Mrs. Ballard gave her no rest until she gave her the most positive assurance that she would part with the maid on her next visit at Natchez. And thus she is found pressing her suit at the residence of the Mississippi planter.

CHAPTER 3
THE FATE OF MAGGIE

After dinner colonel Franks again pressed the inquiry concerning the disposition of his lady. At this time the maid was in the culinary department taking her dinner. The children having been served, she preferred the company of her old mother, whom she loved, the children hanging around and upon her lap. There was no servant save the boy Tony present in the parlor.

"I can't, I won't let her go! she's a dear good girl!" replied Mrs. Franks. "The children are attached to her, and so am I; let Minny or any other of them go—but do not, for Heaven's sake, tear Maggie from me!"

"Maria, my dear, you've certainly lost your balance of mind! Do try and compose yourself," admonished the Colonel. "There's certainly no disposition to do contrary to your desires; try and be a little reasonable."

"I'm sure cousin, I see no cause for your importunity. No one that I know of designs to hurt the negro girl. I'm sure it's not me!" impatiently remarked Mrs. Ballard.

During this, the boy had several times gone into the hall, looking toward the kitchen, then meaningly into the parlor as if something unusual were going on.

Mammy Judy becoming suspicious, went into the hall and stood close beside the parlor door, listening at the conversation.

"Cousin, if you will listen for a moment, I wish to say a word to you," said Mrs. Ballard. "The Judge, as you know, has a country seat

---

1 *jade* Derogatory term for a woman perceived to be rude or poorly behaved.

in Cuba near the city of Havana, where we design making every year our winter retreat. As we cannot take with us either free negroes or white servants, on account of the existing restrictions,[1] I must have a slave, and of course I prefer a well-trained one, as I know all of yours to be. The price will be no object; as I know it will be none to you, it shall be none to me."

"I will not consent to part with her, cousin Arabella, and it is useless to press the matter any further!" emphatically replied Mrs. Franks.

"I am sure, cousin Maria, it was well understood between the Colonel and the Judge, that I was to have one of your best-trained maid servants!" continued Mrs. Ballard.

"The Colonel and the Judge! If any such understanding exist, it is without my knowledge and consent, and—"

"It is true, my dear," interposed the Colonel, "but—"

"Then," replied she, "heaven grant that I may go too! from—"

"Pah, pah! cousin Maria Franks, I'm really astonished at you to take on so about a negro girl! You really appear to have lost your reason. I would not behave so for all the negroes in Mississippi."

"My dear," said Franks, "I have been watching the conduct of that girl for some time past; she is becoming both disobedient and unruly, and as I have made it a rule of my life never to keep a disobedient servant, the sooner we part with her the better. As I never whip my servants, I do not want to depart from my rule in her case."

Maggie was true to her womanhood, and loyal to her mistress, having more than once communicated to her ears facts the sound of which reflected no credit in his. For several repulses, such as this, it was that she became obnoxious to her master.[2]

"Cousin Maria, you certainly have forgotten; I'm sure, when last at the North, you promised, in presence of the girl, that I was to have her, and I'm certain she's expecting it," explained Mrs. Ballard.

"This I admit," replied Mrs. Franks, "but you very well know, cousin Arabella, that that promise was a mere *ruse*, to reconcile an uneasiness which you informed me you discovered in her, after

---

1 *the existing restrictions* Cuba had implemented a ban on free people of color entering the colony in 1844, after an alleged antislavery conspiracy.

2 *Maggie ... her master* The implication is that Maggie had previously rejected Colonel Franks's sexual overtures.

overhearing a conversation between her and some free negroes, at Saratoga Springs."

"Well, cousin, you can do as you please," concluded Mrs. Ballard.

"Colonel, I'm weary of this conversation. What am I to expect?" inquired Mrs. Franks.

"It's a settled point, my dear, she must be sold!" decisively replied Franks.

"Then I must hereafter be disrespected by our own slaves! You know, Colonel, that I gave my word to Henry, her husband, your most worthy servant, that his wife should be here on his return. He had some misgiving that she was to be taken to Cuba before his return, when I assured him that she should be here. How can I bear to meet this poor creature, who places every confidence in what we tell him? He'll surely be frantic."

"Nonsense, cousin, nonsense," sneered Mrs. Ballard; "frantic, indeed! Why you speak of your negro slaves as if speaking of equals. Make him know that whatever you order, he must be contented with."

"I'll soon settle the matter with him, should he dare show any feelings about it!" interposed Franks; "when do you look for him, Maria?"

"I'm sure, Colonel you know more about the matter than I do. Immediately after you left, he took the horses to Baton Rouge, where at the last accounts, he was waiting the conclusion of the races. Judge Dilbreath had entered them according to your request one horse for each day's races. I look for him every day. Then there are more than him to reconcile. There's old mammy Judy, who will run mad about her. You know, Colonel, she thought so much of her, that she might be treated tenderly the old creature gave up her situation in the house as nurse and foster-mother to our children, going into the kitchen to do the harder work."

"Well, my dear, we'll detain your cousin till he comes. I'll telegraph the Judge that if not yet left, to start him home immediately."

"Colonel that will be still worse, to let him witness her departure; I would much rather she'd leave before his return. Poor thing!" she sighed.

"Then she may go!" replied he.

"And what of poor old mammy and his boy?"

"I'll soon settle the matter with old Judy."

Mrs. Franks looking him imploringly in the face, let drop her head, burying her face in the palms of her hands. Soon it was found necessary to place her under the care of a physician.

Old mammy Judy had long since beckoned her daughter, where both stood in breathless silence catching every word that passed.

At the conclusion, Maggie clasping her hands, exclaimed in suppressed tones—

"O mammy, O mammy! what shall I do? O, is there no hope for me? Can't you beg master—can't you save me!"

"Look to de Laud, my chile! him ony able to bring yeh out mo' nah conkeh!"[1] was the prayerful advice of the woe-stricken old mother; both hastening into the kitchen, falling upon their knees, invoked aloud the God of the oppressed.

Hearing in that direction an unusual noise, Franks hastened past the kitchen door, dropping his head, and clearing his throat as he went along. This brought the slaves to an ordinary mood, who trembled at his approach.

CHAPTER 4
DEPARTURE OF MAGGIE

The country-seat of Franks, or the "great house" of the cotton plantation, was but a short distance from the city. Mrs. Franks, by the advice of her physician, was removed there to avoid the disturbance of the town, when at the same time Mrs. Ballard left with her slave Maggie *en route* for Baltimore, whither she designed leaving her until ready to sail for Cuba.

"Fahwell, my chile! fahwell; may God A'mighty be wid you!" were the parting words of the poor old slave, who with streaming eyes gazed upon her parting child for the last time.

"O mammy! can't you save me? O Lord, what shall I do! O my husband! O my poor child! O my! O my!" were the only words, the sounds of which died upon the breeze, as the cab hastily bore her to a steamer then lying at the wharf.

---

1   *mo' nah conkeh*   I.e., more than a conqueror; the allusion is to Romans 8.37: "Nay, in all these things we are more than conquerors through him [Christ] that loved us."

Poor old mammy Judy sat at the kitchen door with elbow resting upon her knee, side of the face resting in the palm of the hand, tears streaming down, with a rocking motion, noticing nothing about her, but in sorrow moaning just distinctly enough to be understood: "Po' me! po' me! po' me!"

The sight was enough to move the heart of anyone, and it so affected Franks, that he wished he had "never owned a negro."

Daddy Joe, the husband of mammy Judy, was a field hand on the cotton place,[1] visiting his wife at the town residence, every Saturday night. Colonel Franks was a fine, grave, senatorial looking man, of medium height, inclined to corpulency, black hair, slightly grey, and regarded by his slaves as a good master, and religiously as one of the best of men.

On their arrival at the great house, those working nearest, gathered around the carriage, among whom was daddy Joe.

"Wat a mautta wid missus?" was the general inquiry of the gang.

"Your mistress is sick, boys," replied the master.

"Maus,[2] whah's Margot?" enquired the old man, on seeing his mistress carried into the house without the attendance of her favorite maid-servant.

"She's in town, Joe," replied Franks.

"How's Judy, seh?"

"Judy is well."

"Tank' e seh!" politely concluded the old man, with a bow, turning away in the direction of his work, with a countenance expressive of anything but satisfaction from the interview.

The slaves, from their condition, are suspicious; any evasion or seeming design at suppressing the information sought by them, frequently arouses their greatest apprehensions.

Not unfrequently the mere countenance, a look, a word, or laugh of the master, is an unerring foreboding of misfortune to the slave. Ever on the watch for these things, they learn to read them with astonishing precision.

This day was Friday, and the old slave consoled himself with the thought that on the next evening he would be able to see and know

---

1   *the cotton place*   I.e., the plantation.
2   *Maus*   Master.

for himself the true state of things about his master's residence in town. The few hours intervening were spent with great anxiety, which was even observed by his fellow-slaves.

At last came Saturday evening and with it, immediately after sunset, daddy Joe made his appearance at the hall door of the great house, tarrying only long enough to inquire "How's missus?" and receive the reply, "she's better," when a few moments found him quite out of sight, striding his way down the lane toward the road to the city.

The sudden and unexpected fate of Maggie had been noised among the slaves throughout the entire neighborhood; many who had the opportunity of doing so, repairing to the house to learn the facts.

In the lower part of the town, bordering on the river there is a depot or receptacle for the slave gangs brought by professional traders. This part of the town is known as "Natchez under the Hill." It is customary among the slaves when any of their number are sold, to say that they are gone "under the hill," and their common salutation through the day was that "Franks' Mag had gone under the hill."

As with quickened steps daddy Joe approached the town, his most fearful apprehensions became terribly realised when meeting a slave who informed him that "Margot had gone under the hill." Falling upon his knees, in the fence corner, the old man raised his voice in supplication of Divine aid:

"O Laud! dow has promis' in dine own wud, to be a fadah to de fadeless, an' husband do de widah![1] O Laud, let dy wud run an' be glorify! Sof'en de haud haut ob de presseh,[2] an' let my po' chile cum back! an'—"

"Stop that noise there, old nigger!"[3] ordered a patrol approaching him; "who's boy are you?"

"Sahvant, mausta!" saluted the old slave, "I b'long to cunel Frank, seh!"

"Is this old Joe?"

"Dis is me maus Johnny."

---

1   *fadah to ... de widah*   See Psalm 68.5: "A father of the fatherless, and a judge of the widows, is God in his holy habitation."

2   *de haud ... presseh*   The hard heart of the oppressor.

3   *nigger*   By the nineteenth century, this word had acquired the extremely derogatory connotations it holds today; nevertheless, it was regularly used.

"You had better trudge along home then, as it's likely old Judy wants to see you about this time."

"Tank'e seh," replied the old man, with a bow, feeling grateful that he was permitted to proceed.

"Devilish good, religious old negro," he remarked to his associates, as the old man left them in the road.

A few minutes more, and daddy Joe entered the kitchen door at his master's residence. Mammy Judy, on seeing him, gave vent afresh to bitter wailing, when the emotion became painfully mutual.

"O husban'! husban'! ouah po' chile is gone!" exclaimed the old woman, clasping him around the neck.

"Laud! dy will be done!" exclaimed he, "ole 'umin,[1] look to de Laud! as he am suffishen fah all tings." Both, falling on their knees, breathed in silence their desires to God.

"How long! how long! O Laud how long!" was the supplicating cry of the old woman, being overcome with devotion and sorrow.

Taking the little grandchild in his arms—"Po' chile," said the old man, "I wish yeh had nebeh been baun!" impressing upon it kisses whilst it slept.

After a fervent and earnest prayer to God for protection to themselves, the little grandson Joe, the return of his mother their only child, and blessings upon their master and the recovery of their mistress, the poor old slaves retired to rest for the evening, to forget their sorrows in the respite of sleep.

Chapter 5
A Vacancy

This morning the sun rose with that beauty known to a southern sky in the last month of autumn. The day was Sabbath, and with it was ushered in every reminiscence common to the customs of that day and locality.

That she might spend the day at church for the diversion of her mind, Mrs. Franks was brought into her city residence; and Natchez, which is usually gay, seemed more so on this day than on former occasions.

---

1 '*umin* Woman.

When the bells began to signalise the hour of worship, the fashionable people seemed *en masse* to crowd the streets. The carriages ran in every direction, bearing happy hearts and cheerful faces to the various places of worship—there to lay their offerings on the altar of The Most High for the blessings they enjoyed, whilst peering over every gate, out of every ally, or every kitchen door, could be seen the faithful black servants, who, staying at home to prepare them food and attend to other domestic duties, were satisfied to look smilingly upon their masters and families as they rode along, without for a moment dreaming that they had a right to worship the same God, with the same promise of life and salvation.

"God bless you, missus! pray fah me," was the honest request of many a simple-hearted slave who dared not aspire to the enjoyment of praying for themselves in the Temple of the living God.

But amidst these scenes of gaiety and pleasure, there was one much devoted to her church, who could not be happy that day, as there, to her, was a seeming vacancy which could not be filled—the seat of her favorite maidservant. The Colonel, as a husband and father, was affectionate and indulgent; but his *slave* had offended, disobeyed his commands, and consequently had to be properly punished, or he be disrespected by his own servants. The will of the master being absolute, his commands should be enforced, let them be what they may, and the consequences what they would. If slavery be right, the master is justifiable in enforcing obedience to his will; deny him this, and you at once deprive him of the right to hold a slave—the one is a necessary sequence of the other. Upon this principle colonel Franks acted, and the premise justified the conclusion.

When the carriage drove to the door, Mrs. Franks wept out most bitterly, refusing to enter because her favorite maid could not be an incumbent. Fears being entertained of seriousness in her case,[1] it was thought advisable to let her remain quietly at home.

Daddy Joe and mammy Judy were anxious spectators of all that transpired at the door of the mansion, and that night, on retiring to their humble bed, earnestly petitioned at the altar of Grace, that the Lord would continue upon her his afflictions, until their master,

---

1   *Fears being … her case*   I.e., it being feared that Mrs. Franks's condition of emotional agitation might be serious.

convinced of his wrongs, would order the return of their child.

This the Colonel would have most willingly done without the petition of Joe or Judy, but the case had gone too far, the offense was too great, and consequently there could be no reconsideration.

"Poor thing," uttered Mrs. Franks in a delirium, "she served him right! And this her only offense! Yes, she was true to me!"

Little Joe, the son of Maggie, in consequence of her position to the white children—from whom her separation had been concealed—had been constantly with his grandmother, and called her "mammy." Accustomed to being without her, he was well satisfied so long as permitted to be with the old woman Judy.

So soon as her condition would permit, Mrs. Franks was returned to her country seat, to avoid the contingencies of the city.

CHAPTER 6
HENRY'S RETURN

Early on Monday morning, a steamer was heard puffing up the Mississippi. Many who reside near the river, by custom can tell the name of every approaching boat by the peculiar sound of the steam-pipe, the one in the present instance being the *Sultana*.[1]

Daddy Joe had risen and [was] just leaving for the plantation, but stopped a moment to be certain.

"Hush!" admonished mammy Judy, "hush! sho chile, do'n yeh heah how she hollah? Sholy dat's de wat's name! wat dat yeh call eh? *Suckana*, wat not; sho! I ain' gwine bautha my head long so—sho! See, ole man see! dah she come! See dat now! I tole yeh so, but yeh uden bleve[2] me!" And the old man and woman stood for some minutes in breathless silence, although the boat must have been some five miles distant, as the escape of steam can be heard on the western waters a great way off.

The approach toward sunrise admonished daddy Joe of demands for him at the cotton farm, when after bidding "good monin' ole umin," he hurried to the daily task which lie before him.

---

1 *the Sultana* Reference to a real steamboat that operated on the Mississippi River in the 1850s. (The original *Sultana* was decommissioned and replaced by a new ship of the same name in 1863; it was that second *Sultana* that infamously exploded in 1865, killing hundreds.)
2 *uden bleve* Wouldn't believe.

Mammy Judy had learned by the boy Tony that Henry was expected on the *Sultana*, and at the approach of every steamer, her head had been thrust out of the door or window to catch a distinct sound. In motionless attitude after the departure of her husband this morning, the old woman stood awaiting the steamer, when presently the boat arrived. But then to be certain that it was the expected vessel—now came the suspense.

The old woman was soon relieved from this most disagreeable of all emotions by the cry of news boys returning from the wharf—

"'Ere's the *Picayune, Atlas, Delta!*[1] lates' news from New Orleans by the swift steamer *Sultana!*"

"Dah now!" exclaimed mammy Judy in soliloquy; "dah now! I tole yeh so! de wat's name come!" Hurrying into the kitchen, she waited with anxiety the arrival of Henry.

Busying about the breakfast for herself and other servants about the house—the white members of the family all being absent—mammy Judy for a time lost sight of the expected arrival. Soon, however, a hasty footstep arrested her attention, when on looking around it proved to be Henry who came smiling up the yard.

"How'd you go mammy! how's Mag' and the boy?" inquired he, grasping the old woman by the hand.

She burst into a flood of tears, throwing herself upon him.

"What is the matter!" exclaimed Henry, "is Maggie dead?"

"No, chile," with increased sobs she replied, "much betteh she wah."

"My God! has she disgraced herself?"[2]

"No, chile, may be betteh she dun so, den she bin heah now an' not sole. Maus Stephen sell eh case she!—I dun'o, reckon dat's da reason!"

"What! Do you tell me mammy she had better disgraced herself than been sold! By the—!"

"So, Henry! yeh ain' gwine swah![3] hope yeh ain' gwine lose yeh 'ligion? Do'n do so; put yeh trus' in de Laud, he is suffishen fah all!"

"Don't tell me about religion! What's religion to me? My wife is sold away from me by a man who is one of the leading members of

---

1   *Picayune ... Delta*   Nineteenth-century New Orleans newspapers *The Times-Picayune, The Daily Atlas,* and *The Daily Delta.*

2   *disgraced herself*   I.e., had sexual relations with—or been raped by—Colonel Franks.

3   *gwine swah*   Going to swear.

the very church to which both she and I belong! Put my trust in the Lord! I have done so all my life nearly, and of what use is it to me? My wife is sold from me just the same as if I didn't. I'll—"

"Come, come, Henry, yeh mus'n talk so; we is po' weak an' bline cretehs, an' cah[1] see de way uh da Laud. He move' in a mystus way, his wundahs to puhfaum."[2]

"So he may, and what is all that to me? I don't gain anything by it, and—"

"Stop, Henry, stop! ain' de Laud bless yo' soul? ain' he take yeh foot out de miah an' clay, an' gib yeh hope da uddah side dis vale ub teahs?"[3]

"I'm tired looking the other side; I want a hope this side of the vale of tears. I want something on this earth as well as a promise of things in another world. I and my wife have been both robbed of our liberty, and you want me to be satisfied with a hope of heaven. I won't do any such thing: I have waited long enough on heavenly promises; I'll wait no longer. I—"

"Henry, wat de mauttah wid yeh? I neveh heah yeh talk so fo'[4]—yeh sin in de sight ub God; yeh gone clean back,[5] I reckon. De good Book tell us, a tousan' yeahs wid man, am but a day wid de Laud.[6] Boy, yeh got wait de Laud own pinted[7] time."

"Well mammy, it is useless for me to stand here and have the same gospel preached into my ears by you, that I have all my lifetime heard from my enslavers. My mind is made up, my course is laid out, and if life last, I'll carry it out. I'll go out to the place today, and let them know that I have returned."

"Sho boy! what yeh gwine do, bun house down? Bettah put yeh trus' in de Laud!" concluded the old woman.

---

1   *bline cretehs* Blind creatures; *cah* Can't.

2   *He move' ... to puhfaum* Reference to a well-known 1773 hymn by English poet William Cowper, originally titled "Light Shining out of Darkness."

3   *he take ... an' clay* See Psalm 40.2: "He brought me up also out of an horrible pit, out of the miry clay, and set my feet upon a rock, and established my goings"; *vale ub teahs* Vale of tears; Christian idiom signifying the world as a site of struggle and tragedy that can be escaped only in the afterlife.

4   *fo'* Foul.

5   *gone clean back* I.e., gone back on your religious faith.

6   *De good Book ... de Laud* See 2 Peter 3.8: "But, beloved, be not ignorant of this one thing, that one day is with the Lord as a thousand years, and a thousand years as one day."

7   *pinted* Appointed.

"You have too much religion, mammy, for me to tell you what I intend doing," said Henry in conclusion.

After taking up his little son, impressing on his lips and cheeks kisses for himself and tears for his mother, the intelligent slave left the abode of the care-worn old woman, for that of his master at the cotton place.

Henry was a black—a pure negro—handsome, manly and intelligent, in size comparing well with his master, but neither so fleshy nor heavy-built in person. A man of good literary attainments—unknown to Col. Franks, though he was aware he could read and write—having been educated in the West Indies, and decoyed[1] away when young. His affection for wife and child was not excelled by colonel Franks for his. He was bold, determined and courageous, but always mild, gentle and courteous, though impulsive when an occasion demanded his opposition.

Going immediately to the place, he presented himself before his master. Much conversation ensued concerning the business which had been entrusted to his charge, all of which was satisfactorily transacted, and full explanations concerning the horses, but not a word was uttered concerning the fate of Maggie, the Colonel barely remarking "your mistress is unwell."

After conversing till a late hour, Henry was assigned a bed in the great house, but sleep was far from his eyes. He turned and changed upon his bed with restlessness and anxiety, impatiently awaiting a return of the morning.

Chapter 7
Master and Slave

Early on Tuesday morning, in obedience to his master's orders, Henry was on his way to the city, to get the house in readiness for the reception of his mistress, Mrs. Franks having much improved in three or four days. Mammy Judy had not yet risen when he knocked at the door.

---

1 *decoyed* Enticed or tricked (i.e., into his present position of slavery).

"Hi Henry! yeh heah ready![1] huccum yeh git up so soon; arter some mischif I reckon? Do'n reckon yeh arter any good!" saluted mammy Judy.

"No mammy," replied he; "no mischief, but like a good slave such as you wish me to be, come to obey my master's will, just what you like to see."

"Sho boy! none yeh nonsens'; huccum I want yeh bey maus Stephen? Git dat nonsens' in yeh head las' night long so, I reckon! Wat dat yeh gwine do now?"

"I have come to dust and air the mansion for their reception. They have sold my wife away from me, and who else would do her work?" This reply excited the apprehension of mammy Judy.

"Wat yeh gwine go Henry? yeh arter no good; yeh ain' gwine 'tack maus Stephen is yeh?"

"What do you mean, mammy, strike him?"

"Yes! reckon yeh ain' gwine hit 'im?"

"Curse—!"

"Henry, Henry, membeh wat ye 'fess?[2] fah de Laud sake, yeh ain gwine take to swahin?"[3] interrupted the old woman.

"I make no profession, mammy. I once did believe in religion, but now I have no confidence in it. My faith has been wrecked on the stony hearts of such pretended Christians as Stephen Franks, while passing through the stormy sea of trouble and oppression! and—"

"Hay, boy! yeh is gittin high! yeh call maussa 'Stephen'?"

"Yes, and I'll never call him 'master' again, except when compelled to do so."

"Bettah g'long ten' t' de house fo' wite folks come, an' nebeh mine talkin' 'bout fightin' 'long wid maus Stephen. Wat yeh gwine do wid white folks? Sho!"

"I don't intend to fight him, mammy Judy, but I'll attack him concerning my wife, if the words be my last! Yes, I'll—!" and pressing his lips to suppress the words, the outraged man turned away from the old slave mother, with such feelings as only an intelligent slave could realize.

---

1   *heah ready*   Here already.
2   *'fess*   Profess; referring to a profession of Christian faith.
3   *swahin*   Swearing.

The orders of the morning were barely executed, when the carriage came to the door. The bright eyes of the foot boy Tony sparkled when he saw Henry approaching the carriage.

"Well Henry! ready for us?" enquired his master.

"Yes sir," was the simple reply. "Mistress!" he saluted, politely bowing as he took her hand to assist her from the carriage.

"Come Henry, my man, get out the riding horses," ordered Franks after a little rest.

"Yes sir."

A horse for the Colonel and lady each was soon in readiness at the door, but none for himself, it always having been the custom in their morning rides, for the maid and manservant to accompany the mistress and master.

"Ready did you say?" enquired Franks on seeing but two horses standing at the stile.

"Yes sir."

"Where's the other horse?"

"What for sir?"

"What for? yourself to be sure!"

"Colonel Franks!" said Henry, looking him sternly in the face, "when I last rode that horse in company with you and lady, *my wife* was at my side, and I will not now go without her! Pardon me—my life for it, I won't go!"

"Not another word you black imp!" exclaimed Franks, with an uplifted staff in a rage, "or I'll strike you down in an instant!"

"Strike away if you will sir, I don't care—I won't go without my wife!"

"You impudent scoundrel! I'll soon put an end to your conduct! I'll put you on the auction block, and sell you to the negro traders."

"Just as soon as you please sir, the sooner the better, as I don't want to live with you any longer!"

"Hold your tongue sir, or I'll cut it out of your head! you ungrateful black dog! Really things have come to a pretty pass, when I must take impudence off my own negro! By gracious! God forgive me for the expression—I'll sell every negro I have first! I'll dispose of him to the hardest negro trader I can find!" said Franks in a rage.

"You may do your mightiest, colonel Franks. I'm not your slave, nor never was, and you know it! and but for my wife and her people, I never would have stayed with you till now. I was decoyed away when young, and then became entangled in such domestic relations as to induce me to remain with you; but now the tie is broken! I know that the odds are against me, but never mind!"

"Do you threaten me, sir! Hold your tongue, or I'll take your life instantly, you villain!"

"No sir, I don't threaten you, colonel Franks, but I do say that I won't be treated like a dog. You sold my wife away from me, after always promising that she should be free. And more than that, you sold her because——! and now you talk about whipping me. Shoot me, sell me, or do anything else you please, but don't lay your hands on me, as I will not suffer you to whip me!"

Running up to his chamber, colonel Franks seized a revolver, when Mrs. Franks, grasping hold of his arm, exclaimed—

"Colonel! what does all this mean?"

"Mean, my dear? It's rebellion! a plot—this is but the shadow of a cloud that's fast gathering around us! I see it plainly, I see it!" responded the Colonel, starting for the stairs.

"Stop, Colonel!" admonished his lady, "I hope you'll not be rash. For Heaven's sake, do not stain your hands in blood!"

"I do not mean to, my dear! I take this for protection!" Franks hastening downstairs, when Henry had gone into the back part of the premises.

"Dah now! dah now!' exclaimed mammy Judy as Henry entered the kitchen, "see wat dis gwine back done foh yeh! Bettah put yo' trus' in de Laud! Henry, yeh gone clean back t'de wuhl,[1] yeh knows it!"

"You're mistaken mammy, I do trust the Lord as much as ever, but I now understand him better than I use to, that's all. I don't intend to be made a fool of any longer by false preaching."

"Henry!" interrogated Daddy Joe, who, apprehending difficulties in the case, had managed to get back to the house, "yeh gwine lose all yo' ligion? Wat yeh mean boy!"

"Religion!" replied Henry rebukingly, "that's always the cry with black people. Tell me nothing about religion when the very man who

---

1 *t'de wuhl* To the world; i.e., to worldly rather than spiritual concerns.

hands you the bread at communion, has sold your daughter away from you!"

"Den yeh 'fen'[1] God case man 'fen' yeh! Take cah Henry, take cah! mine wat yeh 'bout; God is lookin' at yeh, an' if yeh no' willin' trus' 'im, yeh need'n call on 'im in time o' trouble."

"I don't intend, unless He does more for me then than he has done before. 'Time of need!'[2] If ever man needed his assistance, I'm sure I need it now."

"Yeh do'n know wat yeh need; de Laud knows bes'. On'y trus' in 'im, an' 'e bring yeh out mo' nah conkah. By de help o' God I's heah dis day, to gib yeh cumfut!"

"I have trusted in Him daddy Joe, all my life, as I told mammy Judy this morning, but—"

"Ah boy, yeh's gwine back! Dat on't do Henry, dat on't do!"

"Going back from what? my oppressor's religion! If I could only get rid of his inflictions as easily as I can his religion, I would be this day a free man, when you might then talk to me about 'trusting.'"

"Dis Henry, am one uh de ways ob de Laud; 'e fus 'flicks[3] us an' den he bless us."

"Then it's a way I don't like."

"Mine how yeh talk, boy!

God moves in a myst'us way
His wundahs to pehfaum, an—"

"He moves too slow for me daddy Joe; I'm tired waiting so—"

"Come Henry, I hab no such talk like dat! yeh is gittin' rale weaked; yeh gwine let de debil take full 'session on[4] yeh! Take cah boy, mine how yeh talk!"

"It is not wickedness, daddy Joe; you don't understand these things at all. If a thousand years with us is but a day with God, do you think that I am required to wait all that time?"

---

1 *'fen'* Offend.
2 *Time of need* See Hebrews 4.16: "Let us therefore come boldly unto the throne of grace, that we may obtain mercy, and find grace to help in time of need."
3 *'flicks* Afflicts.
4 *weaked* Wicked; *'session on* Possession of.

"Don't Henry, don't! de wud say 'Stan' still an' see de salbation.'"[1]

"That's no talk for me daddy Joe, I've been 'standing still' long enough; I'll 'stand still' no longer."

"Den yeh no call t' bey God wud? Take cah boy, take cah!"

"Yes I have, and I intend to obey it, but that part was intended for the Jews, a people long since dead. I'll obey that intended for me."

"How yeh gwine bey it?"

"'Now is the accepted time, today is the day of salvation.'[2] So you see, daddy Joe, this is very different to standing still."

"Ah boy, I's feahd yeh's losen yeh 'ligion!"

"I tell you once for all daddy Joe, that I'm not only 'losing,' but I have altogether lost my faith in the religion of my oppressors. As they are our religious teachers, my estimate of the thing they give, is no greater than it is for those who give it."

With elbows upon his knees, and face resting in the palms of his hands, daddy Joe for some time sat with his eyes steadily fixed on the floor, whilst Ailcey, who for a part of the time had been an auditor to the conversation, went into the house about her domestic duties.

"Never mind, Henry! I hope it will not always be so with you. You have been kind and faithful to me and the Colonel, and I'll do anything I can for you!" sympathetically said Mrs. Franks, who having been a concealed spectator of the interview between Henry and the old people, had just appeared before them.

Wiping away the emblems of grief which stole down his face, with a deep-toned voice, upgushing from the recesses of a more than iron-pierced soul, he enquired—

"Madam, what can you do! Where is my wife?" To this, Mrs. Franks gave a deep sigh. "Never mind, never mind!" continued he, "yes, I will mind, and by—!"

"O! Henry, I hope you've not taken to swearing! I do hope you will not give over to wickedness! Our afflictions should only make our faith the stronger."

"'Wickedness!' Let the righteous correct the wicked, and the Christian condemn the sinner!"

---

1 *Stan' still ... salbation* Words said by Moses to the Israelites before their departure from Egyptian slavery; see Exodus 14.13.

2 *Now is ... of salvation* See 2 Corinthians 6.2.

"That is uncharitable in you Henry! as you know I have always treated you kindly, and God forbid that I should consider myself any less than a Christian! and I claim as much at least for the Colonel, though like frail mortals he is liable to err at times."

"Madam!" said he with a suppressed emotion—starting back a pace or two—"do you think there is anything either in or out of hell so wicked, as that which colonel Franks has done to my wife, and now about to do to me? For myself I care not—my wife!"

"Henry!" said Mrs. Franks, gently placing her hand upon his shoulder, "there is yet a hope left for you, and you will be faithful enough I know, not to implicate any person; it is this: Mrs. Van Winter, a true friend of your race, is shortly going to Cuba on a visit, and I will arrange with her to purchase you through an agent on the day of your sale, and by that means you can get to Cuba, where probably you may be fortunate enough to get the master of your wife to become your purchaser."

"Then I have two chances!" replied Henry.

Just then Ailcey, thrusting her head in the door, requested the presence of her mistress in the parlor.

CHAPTER 8
THE SALE

"Dah now, dah now!" exclaimed mammy Judy; "jis wat ole man been tellin' on yeh! Yeh go out yandah, yeh kick up yeh heel, git yeh head clean full proclamation an' sich like dat, an' let debil fool yeh, den go fool long wid wite folks long so, sho! Bettah go 'bout yeh bisness; been sahvin' God right, yeh no call t'do so eh reckon!"

"I don't care what comes! my course is laid out and my determination fixed, and nothing they can do can alter it. So you and daddy Joe, mammy, had just as well quit your preaching to me the religion you have got from your oppressors."

"Soul-driveh[1] git yeh, yeh cah git way fom dem eh doh recken! Sho chile, yeh, ain' dat mighty!" admonished mammy Judy.

"Henry my chile, look to de Laud! look to de Laud! case 'e 'lone am able t' bah us up in ouah[2] trouble! an—"

---

1   *Soul-driveh*   Person who works in the transport and sale of enslaved people.
2   *'e 'lone … in ouah*   He alone is able to bear us up in our.

"Go directly sir, to captain John Harris' office and ask him to call immediately to see me at my house!" ordered Franks.

Politely bowing, Henry immediately left the premises on his errand.

"Laud a' messy[1] maus Stephen!" exclaimed mammy Judy, on hearing the name of John Harris the negro-trader; "hope yeh arteh no haum! gwine sell all on us to de tradehs?"

"Hoot-toot, hoot-toot! Judy, give yourself no uneasiness about that, till you have some cause for it. So you and Joe may rest contented Judy," admonished Franks.

"Tank'e maus Stephen! case ah heahn yeh tell Henry dat yeh sell de las' nig—"

"Hush! ole umin, hush! yeh tongue too long! Put yeh trus' in de Laud!" interrupted daddy Joe.

"I treat my black folks well," replied Franks; "and all they have to—"

Here the doorbell having been rung, he was interrupted with a message from Ailcey, that a gentleman awaited his presence in the parlor.

At the moment which the Colonel left the kitchen, Henry stepped over the stile into the yard, which at once disclosed who the gentleman was to whom the master had been summoned. Henry passed directly around and behind the house.

"See, ole man, see! reckon 'e gwine dah now!" whispered mammy Judy, on seeing Henry pass through the yard without going into the kitchen.

"Whah?" enquired daddy Joe.

"Dun'o out yandah, whah 'e gwine way from wite folks!" she replied.

The interview between Franks and the trader Harris was not over half an hour duration, the trader retiring, Franks being prompt and decisive in all of his transactions, making little ceremony.

So soon as the front door was closed, Ailcey smiling bore into the kitchen a half pint glass of brandy, saying that her master had sent it to the old people.

---

1 *messy* Mercy.

The old man received it with compliments to his master, pouring it into a black jug in which there was both tansy and garlic, highly recommending it as a "bitters" and certain antidote for worms, for which purpose he and the old woman took of it as long as it lasted, though neither had been troubled with that particular disease since the days of their childhood.

"Wat de gwine do wid yeh meh son?" enquired mammy Judy as Henry entered the kitchen.

"Sell me to the soul-drivers! what else would they do?"

"Yeh gwin 'tay 'bout till de git yeh?"

"I shan't move a step! and let them do their—!"

"Maus wants to see yeh in da front house Henry," interrupted Ailcey, he immediately obeying the summons.

"Heah dat now!" said mammy Judy, as Henry followed the maid out of the kitchen.

"Carry this note sir, directly to captain Jack Harris!" ordered Franks, handing to Henry a sealed note. Receiving it, he bowed politely, going out of the front door, directly to the slave prison of Harris.

"Eh heh! I see," said Harris on opening the note; "colonel Frank's boy; walk in here"; passing through the office into a room which proved to be the first department of the slave-prison. "No common negro I see! you're a shade higher. A pretty deep shade too! Can read, write, cipher;[1] a good religious fellow, and has a Christian[2] and sur-name. The devil you say! Who's your father! Can you preach?"

"I have never tried," was the only reply.

"Have you ever been a member of Congress?" continued Harris with ridicule.

To this Henry made no reply.

"Won't answer hey! beneath your dignity. I understand that you're of that class of gentry who don't speak to common folks! You're not quite well enough dressed for a gentleman of your cloth. Here! Mr. Henry, I'll present you with a set of ruffles: give yourself no trouble sir, as I'll dress you! I'm here for that purpose," said Harris, fastening upon the wrists of the manly bondman a heavy pair of handcuffs.

---

1 *cipher* I.e., calculate; do arithmetic.
2 *Christian* First (name).

"You hurt my wrist!" admonished Henry.

"New clothing will be a little tight when first put on. Now sir!" continued the trader, taking him to the back door and pointing into the yard at the slave gang there confined; "as you have been respectably dressed, walk out and enjoy yourself among the ladies and gentlemen there; you'll find them quite a select company."

Shortly after this the sound of the bell-ringer's voice was heard—a sound which usually spread terror among the slaves: "Will be sold this afternoon at three o'clock by public outcry, at the slave-prison of captain John Harris, a likely choice negro-fellow, the best trained body servant in the state, trained to the business by the most accomplished lady and gentleman negro-trainers in the Mississippi Valley. Sale positive without a proviso."[1]

"Dah, dah! did'n eh tell yeh so? Ole man, ole man! heah dat now! Come heah. Dat jis what I been tellin on im, but 'e uden blieve me!" ejaculated old mammy Judy on hearing the bell ring and the hand bill read.

Falling upon their knees, the two old slaves prayed fervently to God, thanking him that it was as "well with them" as it was.

"Bless de Laud! my soul is happy!" cried out mammy Judy, being overcome with devotion, clapping her hands.

"Tang God, fah wat I feels in my soul!" responded daddy Joe.

Rising from their knees with tears trickling down their cheeks, the old slaves endeavored to ease their troubled souls by singing—

Oh, when shall my sorrows subside,
And when shall my troubles be ended;
And when to the bosom of Christ be conveyed,
To the mansions of joy and bliss;
To the mansions of joy and bliss![2]

"Wuhthy to be praise! blessed be de name uh de Laud! Po' black folks, de Laud o'ny knows wats t' come ob us!" exclaimed mammy Judy.

---

1 *Sale positive … proviso* Phrase describing an auction in which the seller is obligated to complete a sale to the highest bidder (as opposed to an auction in which the seller may choose to back out of the sale).

2 *Oh, when … and bliss* Lines of a Christian hymn; in most published versions, the last line of the stanza quoted is rendered as "mansions of glory and peace."

"Look to de Laud ole umin, 'e's able t' bah us out mo' neh conkeh. Keep de monin stah[1] in sight!" advised daddy Joe.

"Yes ole man, yes, dat I is done dis many long day, an' ah ain' gwine lose sight uh it now! No, God bein' my helpeh, I is gwine keep my eyes right on it, dat I is!"

As the hour of three drew near, many there were going in the direction of the slave-prison, a large number of persons having assembled at the sale.

"Draw near, gentlemen! draw near!" cried Harris; "the hour of sale is arrived; a positive sale with no proviso, cash down, or no sale at all!" A general laugh succeeded the introduction of the auctioneer.

"Come up here my lad!" continued the auctioneer, wielding a long red rawhide;[2] "mount this block, stand beside me, an' let's see which is the best-looking man! We have met before, but I never had the pleasure of introducing you. Gentlemen one and all, I take pleasure in introducing to you Henry—pardon me sir—Mr. Henry Holland, I believe—am I right sir?—Mr. Henry Holland, a good looking fellow you will admit.

"I am offered one thousand dollars; one thousand dollars for the best-looking negro in all Mississippi! If all the negro boys in the state was as good looking as him, I'd give two thousand dollars as him, I'd give two thousand dollars for 'em all myself!" This caused another laugh. "Who'll give me one thousand five—"

Just then a shower of rain came on.

"Gentlemen!" exclaimed the auctioneer; "without a place can be obtained large enough to shelter the people here assembled, the sale will have to be postponed. This is a proviso we couldn't foresee, an' therefore is not responsible for it." There was another hearty laugh.

A whisper went through the crowd, when presently a gentleman came forward saying that those concerned had kindly tendered the use of the Church which stood near by, in which to continue the sale.

"Here we are again, gentlemen! Who bids five hundred more for the likely negro fellow? I am offered fifteen hundred dollars for the finest negro servant in the state! Come, my boy, bestir yourself an'

---

1   *monin stah* Morning star; see Revelation 22.16, where Jesus describes himself as "the bright and morning star."
2   *rawhide* I.e., a whip.

don't stan' there like a statue; can't you give us a jig? whistle us a song! I forgot, the negro fellow is religious; by the by, an excellent recommendation gentlemen. Perhaps he'll give us a sermon. Say, git up there old fellow, an' hold forth. Can't you give us a sermon on Abolition? I'm only offered fifteen hundred dollars for the likely negro boy! Fifteen, sixteen, sixteen hundred dollars, seventeen hundred, just agoing at—eighteen, eighteen, nineteen hundred, nineteen nineteen! Just agoing at nineteen hundred dollars for the best body servant in the State; just agoing at nineteen and without a better bid I'll—going! going! go—!"

Just at this point a note was passed up the aisle to the auctioneer, who after reading it said:

"Gentlemen! circumstances beyond my control make it necessary that the sale be postponed until one day next week; the time of continuance will be duly announced," when bowing he left the stand.

"That's another proviso not in the original bill!" exclaimed a voice as the auctioneer left the stand, at which there were peals of laughter.

To secure himself against contingency, Harris immediately delivered Henry over to Franks.

There were present at the sale, Crow, Slider, Walker, Borbridge, Simpson, Hurst, Spangler and Williams, all noted slave traders, eager to purchase, some on their return home, and some with their gangs *en route* for the southern markets.

The note handed the auctioneer read thus:

CAPT. HARRIS—Having learned that there are private individuals at the sale, who design purchasing my negro man, Harry, for his own *personal advantage*, you will peremptorily postpone the sale—making such apology as the occasion demands—and effect a private sale with Richard Crow, Esq., who offers me two thousand dollars for him. Let the boy return to me. Believe me to be,
Very respectfully,
STEPHEN FRANKS
Capt. John Harris
Natchez, Nov. 29th, 1852

"Now sir," said Franks to Henry, who had barely reached the house from the auction block; "take this pass and go to Jackson and Woodville, or anywhere else you wish to see your friends, so that you be back against Monday afternoon. I ordered a postponement of the sale, thinking that I would try you awhile longer, as I never had cause before to part with you. Now see if you can't be a better boy!"

Eagerly taking the note, thanking him with a low bow, turning away, Henry opened the paper, which read:

Permit the bearer my boy Henry, sometimes calling himself Henry Holland—a kind of negro pride he has—to pass and repass wherever he wants to go, he behaving himself properly.

STEPHEN FRANKS

To all whom it may concern.
Natchez, Nov. 29th 1852

Carefully depositing the *charte volante*[1] in his pocket wallet, Henry quietly entered the hut of mammy Judy and daddy Joe.

[In the following chapter, Henry discovers that Franks has sold him to Richard Crow, and that the pass Franks has given him is merely a ruse to have Henry kidnapped. The discovery spurs Henry to escape slavery and declare himself a free man; he makes plans to have his son taken to Canada, while he himself determines to travel through the South and spread the word of revolution among the enslaved population. He implores Mammy Judy and Daddy Joe to escape to Canada as well, but they refuse, protesting that they are too old to make the journey or to adapt to a new life. It is revealed that Henry has amassed substantial savings by taking small amounts of money from Colonel Franks over the years.

Before his departure, Henry calls a secret meeting with two enslaved friends, Andy and Charles.]

CHAPTER II

THE SHADOW

"Ah, boys! here you are, true to your promise," said Henry, as he entered a covert[2] in the thicket adjacent the cotton place, late on Sunday evening, "have you been waiting long?"

"Not very," replied Andy, "not mo' dan two-three ouahs."

---

1 *charte volante* French: loose sheet.
2 *covert* Sheltered area.

"I was fearful you would not come, or if you did before me, that you would grow weary, and leave."

"Yeh no call to doubt us Henry, case yeh fine us true as ole steel!"

"I know it," answered he, "but you know, Andy, that when a slave is once sold at auction, all respect for him—"

"O pshaw! we ain' goin' to heah nothin' like dat a tall! case—"

"No!" interrupted Charles, "all you got to do, Henry, is to tell we boys what you want, an' we're your men."

"That's the talk for me!"

"Well, what you doin' here?" enquired Charles.

"W'at brought yeh back from Jackson so soon?" further enquired Andy.

"How did you get word to meet me here?"

"By Ailcey; she give me the stone,[1] an' I give it to Andy, an' we both sent one apiece back. Didn't you git 'em?"

"Yes, that's the way I knew you intended to meet me," replied Henry.

"So we thought," said Charles, "but tell us, Henry, what you want us to do."

"I suppose you know all about the sale, that they had me on the auction block, but ordered a postponement, and—"

"That's the very pint we can't understand, although I'm in the same family with you,"[2] interrupted Charles.

"But tell us Henry, what yeh doin' here?" impatiently enquired Andy.

"Yes," added Charles, "we want to know."

"Well, I'm a *runaway*, and from this time forth, I swear—I do it religiously—that I'll never again serve any white man living!"

"That's the pint I wanted to git at before," explained Charles, "as I can't understan' why you run away, after your release from Jack Harris, an'—"

"Nah I, nuthah!" interrupted Andy.

---

1 *she give me the stone* Presumably a device used to communicate messages without the knowledge of one's enslavers.

2 *although I'm ... with you* The exact meaning here is unclear, though the implication seems to be that Charles considers himself and Henry to be akin to family members, and is thus surprised not to instinctively understand Henry's situation.

"It seems to me," continued Charles, "that I'd 'ave went before they 'tempted to sell me, an' that you're safer now than before they had you on the block."

"Dat's da way I look at it," responded Andy.

"The stopping of the sale was to deceive his wife, mammy, and Daddy Joe, as he had privately disposed of me to a regular soul-driver by the name of Crow."

"I knows Dick Crow," said Andy, "'e come f'om Faginy, whah I did, da same town."

"So Ailcey said of him. Then you know him without any description from me," replied Henry.

"Yes 'n deed! an' I knows 'im to be a inhuman, mean, dead-po'[1] white man, dat's wat I does."

"Well, I was privately sold to him for two thousand dollars, then ordered back to Franks, as though I was still his slave, and by him given a pass, and requested to go to Woodville where there were arrangements to seize me and hold me, till Crow ordered me, which was to have been on Tuesday evening. Crow is not aware of me having been given a pass; Franks gave it to deceive his wife, in case of my not returning, to make the impression that I had run away, when in reality I was sold to the trader."

"Then our people had their merrymaking[2] all for nothin'," said Charles, "an' Franks got what 'e didn't deserve—their praise."

"No, the merrymaking was only to deceive Franks, that I might have time to get away. Daddy Joe, Mammy Judy, and Ailcey knew all about it, and proposed the feast to deceive him."

"Dat's good! sarve 'im right, da 'sarned ole scamp!" rejoined Andy.

"It couldn't be better!" responded Charles.

"Henry, uh wish we was in yo' place an' you none da wus by it," said Andy.

"Never mind, boys, give yourselves no uneasiness, as it won't be long before we'll all be together."

"You think so, Henry?" asked Charles.

---

1 *dead-po'* Dead poor.
2 *their merrymaking* In Chapter 10, "Merry Making," Mammy Judy and Daddy Joe host a celebration meant in part to hide the fact that they know about Henry's sale to Crow—and to distract Franks while Henry begins his escape.

"Well uh hope so, but den body can haudly 'spect it," responded Andy.

"Boys," said Henry, with great caution, and much emotion, "I am now about to approach an important subject, and as I have always found you true to me—and you can only be true to me by being true to yourselves—I shall not hesitate to impart it! But for Heaven's sake!—perhaps I had better not!"

"Keep nothin' back, Henry," said Charles, "as you know that we boys 'll die by our principles, that's settled!"

"Yes, I wants to die right now by mine; right heah, now!" sanctioned Andy.

"Well it is this—close, boys! close!" When they gathered in a huddle beneath an underbush, upon their knees, "you both go with me, but not now. I—"

"Why not now?" anxiously enquired Charles.

"Dat's wat I like to know!" responded Andy.

"Stop, boys, till I explain. The plans are mine and you must allow me to know more about them than you. Just here, for once, the slave-holding preacher's advice to the black man is appropriate, 'Stand still and see the salvation.'"

"Then let us hear it, Henry," asked Charles.

"Fah God sake!" said Andy, "let us heah w'at it is, anyhow, Henry; yeh keep a body in 'spence so long, till I's mose crazy to heah it. Dat's no way!"

"You shall have it, but I approach it with caution! Nay, with fear and trembling,[1] at the thought of what has been the fate of all previous matters of this kind. I approach it with religious fear, and hardly think us fit for the task; at least, I know I am not. But as no one has ever originated, or given us anything of the kind, I suppose I may venture."

"Tell it! tell it!" urged both in a whisper.

"Andy," said Henry, "let us have a word of prayer first!" When they bowed low, with their heads to the ground, Andy, who was a preacher of the Baptist persuasion among his slave brethren, offering a solemn and affecting prayer, in whispers to the Most High, to give them knowledge and courage in the undertaking, and success in the effort.

---

1 *with fear and trembling* See Philippians 2.12: "Wherefore, my beloved, as ye have always obeyed, not as in my presence only, but now much more in my absence, work out your own salvation with fear and trembling."

Rising from their knees, Andy commenced an anthem, by which he appeared to be much affected, in the following words:

About our future destiny,
There need be none debate—
Whilst we ride on the tide,
With our Captain and his mate.[1]

Clasping each other by the hand, standing in a band together, as a plight of their union and fidelity to each other, Henry said, "I now impart to you the secret, it is this: I have laid a scheme, and matured a plan for a general insurrection of the slaves in every State, and the successful overthrow of slavery!"

"Amen!" exclaimed Charles.

"God grant it!" responded Andy.

"Tell us, Henry, how's dis to be carried out?" enquired Andy.

"That's the thing which most concerns me, as it seems that it would be hard to do in the present ignorant state of our people in the slave States," replied Charles.

"Dat's jis wat I feah!" said Andy.

"This difficulty is obviated. It is so simple that the most stupid among the slaves will understand it as well as if he had been instructed for a year."

"What!" exclaimed Charles.

"Let's heah dat again!" asked Andy.

"It is so just as I told you! So simple is it that the trees of the forest or an orchard illustrate it; flocks of birds or domestic cattle, fields of corn, hemp or sugar cane; tobacco, rice or cotton, the whistling of the wind, rustling of the leaves, flashing of lightning, roaring of thunder, and running of streams all keep it constantly before their eyes and in their memory, so that they can't forget it if they would."

"Are we to know it now?" enquired Charles.

"I'm boun' to know it dis night befo' I goes home, 'case I been longin' fah ole Pottah[2] dis many day, an' uh mos' think uh got 'im now!"

"Yes boys, you've to know it before we part, but—"

---

1   *About our ... his mate* Lines from the hymn "The People Called Christians."

2   *ole Pottah* Charles and Andy's enslaver, the slaveholder Potter.

"That's the talk!" said Charles.

"Good nuff talk fah me!" responded Andy.

"As I was about to say, such is the character of this organization, that punishment and misery are made the instruments for its propagation, so—"

"I can't understan' that part—"

"You know nothing at all about it Charles, and you must—"

"Stan' still an' see da salvation!" interrupted Andy.

"Amen!" responded Charles.

"God help you so to do, brethren!" admonished Henry.

"Go on Henry tell us! give it to us!" they urged.

"Every blow you receive from the oppressor impresses the organization upon your mind, making it so clear that even Whitehead's Jack[1] could understand it as well as his master."

"We are satisfied! The secret, the secret!" they importuned.

"Well then, first to prayer, and then to the organization. Andy!" said Henry, nodding to him, when they again bowed low with their heads to the ground, whilst each breathed a silent prayer, which was ended with "Amen" by Andy.

Whilst yet upon their knees, Henry imparted to them the secrets of his organization.

"O, dat's da thing!" exclaimed Andy.

"Capital, capital!" responded Charles. "What fools we was that we didn't know it long ago!"

"I is mad wid myse'f now!" said Andy.

"Well, well, well! Surely God must be in the work," continued Charles.

"'E's heah; Heaven's nigh! Ah feels it! It's right heah!" responded Andy, placing his hand upon his chest, the tears trickling down his cheeks.

"Brethren," asked Henry, "do you understand it?"

"Understand it? Why, a child could understand, it's so easy!" replied Charles.

"Yes," added Andy, "ah not only undehstan' myse'f, but wid da knowledge I has uv it, ah could make Whitehead's Jack a Moses!"

---

1   *Whitehead's Jack*   Probably a reference to English writer Charles Whitehead's novel *The Autobiography of Jack Ketch* (1835), about a famously brutal executioner.

"Stand still, then, and see!" said he.

"Dat's good Bible talk!" responded Andy.

"Well, what is we to do?" enquired Charles.

"You must now go on and organize continually. It makes no difference when, nor where you are, so that the slaves are true and trustworthy, as the scheme is adapted to all times and places."

"How we gwine do Henry, 'bout gittin' da things 'mong da boys?" enquired Andy.

"All you have to do, is to find one good man or woman—I don't care which, so that they prove to be the right person—on a single plantation, and hold a seclusion and impart the secret to them, and make them the organizers for their own plantation, and they in like manner impart it to some other next to them, and so on. In this way it will spread like smallpox among them."

"Henry, you is fit fah leadah ah see," complimentingly said Andy.

"I greatly mistrust myself, brethren, but if I can't command, I can at least plan."

"Is they anything else for us to do Henry?" enquired Charles.

"Yes, a very important part of your duties has yet to be stated. I now go as a runaway, and will be suspected of lurking about in the thickets, swamps and caves; then to make the ruse complete, just as often as you think it necessary, to make a good impression, you must kill a shoat, take a lamb, pig, turkey, goose, chickens, ham of bacon from the smoke house, a loaf of bread or crock of butter from the spring house, and throw them down into the old waste well at the back of the old quarters, always leaving the heads of the fowls lying about and the blood of the larger animals. Everything that is missed do not hesitate to lay it upon me, as a runaway, it will only cause them to have the less suspicion of your having such a design."

"That's it—the very thing!" said Charles, "an it so happens that they's an ole waste well on both Franks' and Potter's places, one for both of us."

"I hope Andy, you have no religious objections to this?"

"It's a paut ah my 'ligion, Henry, to do whateveh I bleve right, an' shall sholy do dis, God being my helpah!"

"Now he's talkin'!" said Charles.

"You must make your religion subserve your interests, as your oppressors do theirs!" advised Henry. "They use the Scriptures to make you submit, by preaching to you the texts of 'obedience to your masters'[1] and 'standing still to see the salvation,' and we must now begin to understand the Bible so as to make it of interest to us."

"Dat's gospel talk," sanctioned Andy. "Is da anything else yeh want tell us boss—I calls 'im *boss*, 'case 'e aint nothing else but 'boss'—so we can make 'ase an' git to wuck? 'case I feels like goin' at 'em now, me!"

"Having accomplished our object, I think I have done, and must leave you tomorrow."

"When shall we hear from you, Henry?" enquired Charles.

"Not until you shall see me again; when that will be, I don't know. You may see me in six months, and might not in eighteen. I am determined, now that I am driven to it, to complete an organization in every slave state before I return, and have fixed two years as my utmost limit."

"Henry, tell me before we part, do you know anything about little Joe?" enquired Charles.

"I do!"

"Wha's da chile?" enquired Andy.

"He's safe enough, on his way to Canada!" at which Charles and Andy laughed.

"Little Joe is on 'is way to Canada?" said Andy, "mighty young travelah!"

"Yes," replied Henry with a smile.

"You're a joking, Henry?" said Charles, enquiringly.

"I am serious, brethren," replied he. "I do not joke in matters of this kind. I smiled because of Andy's surprise."

"How did 'e go?" farther enquired Andy.

"In company with his 'mother' who was waiting on her 'mistress!'" replied he quaintly.

"Eh heh!" exclaimed Andy. "I knows all 'bout it now; but whah'd da 'mammy' come f'om?"

"I found one!"

"Aint 'e high!" said Andy.

---

1   *obedience to your masters* Various biblical passages exhort the faithful to obey their enslavers, including Ephesians 6.5: "Slaves, obey your earthly masters with respect and fear, and with sincerity of heart, just as you would obey Christ." See also Colossians 3.22, Titus 2.9, and 1 Peter 2.18.

"Well, brethren, my time is drawing to a close," said Henry, rising to his feet.

"O!" exclaimed Andy, "ah like to forgot, has yeh any money Henry?"

"Have either of you any?"

"We has."

"How much?"

"I got two-three hundred dollahs!" replied Andy.

"An' so has I, Henry!" added Charles.

"Then keep it, as I have two thousand dollars now around my waist, and you'll find use for all you've got, and more, as you will before long have an opportunity of testing. Keep this studiously in mind and impress it as an important part of the scheme of organization, that they must have money, if they want to get free. Money will obtain them everything necessary by which to obtain their liberty. The money is within all of their reach if they only knew it was right to take it. God told the Egyptian slaves to 'borrow from their neighbors'—meaning their oppressors—'all their jewels'; meaning to take their money and wealth wherever they could lay hands upon it, and depart from Egypt.[1] So you must teach them to take all the money they can get from their masters, to enable them to make the strike without a failure. I'll show you when we leave for the North, what money will do for you, right here in Mississippi. Bear this in mind; it is your certain *passport* through the *white gap*, as I term it."

"I means to take all ah can git; I bin doin' dat dis some time. Ev'ry time ole Pottah leave 'is money pus,[2] I borrys some, an' 'e all'as lays it on Miss Mary, but 'e think so much uh huh, dat anything she do is right wid 'im. Ef 'e 'spected me, an' Miss Mary say 'twant me, dat would be 'nough fah 'im."

"That's right!" said Henry, "I see you have been putting your own interpretation on the Scriptures, Andy, and as Charles will now have to take my place, he'll have still a much better opportunity than you, to 'borrow from his master.'"

"You needn't fear, I'll make good use of my time!" replied Charles.

---

1   *God told ... depart from Egypt*   See Exodus 3.22.
2   *pus*   Purse.

The slaves now fell upon their knees in silent communion, all being affected to the shedding of tears, a period being put to their devotion by a sorrowful trembling of Henry's voice singing to the following touching words:

Farewell, farewell, farewell!
My loving friends farewell!
Farewell old comrades in the cause,
I leave you here, and journey on;
And if I never more return,
Farewell, I'm bound to meet you there![1]

"One word before we part," said Charles. "If we never should see you again, I suppose you intend to push on this scheme?"
"Yes!"

Insurrection shall be my theme!
My watchword "Freedom or the grave!"
Until from Rappahannock's stream,[2]
To where the Cuato[3] waters lave,
One simultaneous war cry
Shall burst upon the midnight air!
And rouse the tyrant but to sigh—
Mid sadness, wailing, and despair!

Grasping each eagerly by the hand, the tears gushing from his eyes, with an humble bow, he bid them finally "farewell!" and the runaway was off through the forest.

—1859

---

1   *Farewell ... you there*   These words, Delany's own, follow the structure of the folk hymn "The Minister's Farewell."
2   *Rappahannock's stream*   The Rappahannock River in Virginia.
3   [Delany's note]   A river in Cuba.

INDEX TO VOLUME I.

Index to *The Anglo-African Magazine*, Volume 1, 1859. The first portion of *Blake* appeared in this volume of the periodical, to which Delany also contributed articles on astronomy.

In Context

Martin R. Delany and Frederick Douglass Debate Harriet Beecher Stowe

Martin R. Delany had a complex relationship with the prominent abolitionist and writer Frederick Douglass; the two men briefly collaborated on the important abolitionist newspaper the *North Star*, but they frequently and often vehemently disagreed on a number of issues related to black liberation. One lightning rod for these issues was Harriet Beecher Stowe, whose phenomenally popular novel *Uncle Tom's Cabin* (1852) had catapulted her to prominence as a spokesperson of the abolitionist cause. Delany was among the number of black intellectuals who were openly wary about the merits of *Uncle Tom's Cabin*—and about positioning Stowe, a white woman, as a leader in black activism—while Douglass was among the most vocal African American supporters of *Uncle Tom's Cabin* and of Stowe herself.

The following selections are from an epistolary exchange between the two men that Douglass published in his newspaper *Frederick Douglass' Paper* in 1853. This exchange not only suggests the ways in which Delany and Douglass sometimes refined their positions by debating each other, but also hints at a similar mutual influence between Delany and Stowe. Her reading of arguments such as those Delany makes below prompted Stowe to put forward a more radical view of the struggle against slavery in her next novel, *Dred: A Tale of the Great Dismal Swamp* (1856). At the same time, Delany's novel *Blake* can in many respects be read as an argument against the ideas put forward in *Uncle Tom's Cabin*, especially the implication that enslaved people should meet the oppression of slavery with passive endurance.

FREDERICK DOUGLASS, ESQ: DEAR SIR: I notice in your paper of March 4th, an article in which you speak of having paid a visit to Mrs. H. E. B. Stowe, for the purpose, as you say, of consulting her, "as to some method which should contribute successfully, and permanently, to the improvement and elevation of the free people of color in the United States."[1] Also, in the number of March 18th, in an article by a writer over the initials of "P.C.S." in reference to the same subject, he concludes by saying, "I await with much interest the suggestions of Mrs. Stowe in this matter."

Now I simply wish to say that we have always fallen into great errors in efforts of this kind, going to others than the *intelligent* and *experienced* among *ourselves*, and in all due respect and deference to Mrs. Stowe, I beg leave to say that she *knows nothing about us*, "the Free Colored people of the United States," neither does any other white person—and, consequently, can contrive no successful scheme for our elevation; it must be done by ourselves. I am aware, that I differ with many in thus expressing myself, but I cannot help it; though I stand alone, and offend my best friends, so help me God! in a matter of such moment and importance, I will express my opinion. Why, in God's name, don't the leaders among our people make suggestions, and *consult* the most competent among *their own* brethren concerning our elevation? This they do not do; and I have not known one, whose province it was to do so, to go ten miles for such a purpose. We shall never effect anything until this is done.

I accord with the suggestions of H.O. Wagoner[2] for a National Council or Consultation of our people, provided *intelligence, maturity*, and *experience*, in matters among them, could be so gathered together; other than this, would be a mere mockery—like the Convention of 1848,[3] a coming together of rivals, to test their success for

---

1 *your paper … United States* Delany refers to the article published in *Frederick Douglass' Paper* as "A Day and Night in 'Uncle Tom's Cabin,'" in which Douglass reflects on a visit paid to Stowe's home in Massachusetts.

2 *H.O. Wagoner* Abolitionist Henry O. Wagoner (1816–1901), a frequent correspondent of Douglass's, who had proposed such a National Council in *Frederick Douglass' Paper* for March 18, 1853.

3 *Convention of 1848* I.e., the Colored National Convention held in Cleveland, Ohio on September 6, attended by both Douglass and Delany.

the "biggest offices." As God lives, I will never, knowingly, lend my aid to any such work, while our brethren groan in vassalage[1] and bondage, and I and mine under oppression and degradation, such as we now suffer.

I would not give the counsel of one dozen *intelligent colored* freemen of the *right stamp*, for that of all the white and unsuitable colored persons in the land. But something must be done, and that speedily.

The so-called free states, by their acts,[2] are now virtually saying to the South, "you *shall not* emancipate; your blacks *must be slaves*, and should they come North, there is no refuge for them." I shall not be surprised to see, at no distant day, a solemn Convention called by the whites in the North, to deliberate on the propriety of changing the whole policy to that of slave states. This will be the remedy to prevent dissolution; *and it will come, mark that!* anything on the part of the American people to *save* their *Union*. Mark me—the non-slaveholding states *will become slave states*.

Yours for God and Humanity.

M.R. DELANY

[1 April 1853]

REMARKS—That colored men would agree among themselves to do something for the efficient and permanent aid of themselves and their race, "is a consummation devoutly to be wished";[3] but until they do, it is neither wise nor graceful for them, or for any one of them to throw cold water upon plans and efforts made for that purpose by others. To scornfully reject all aid from our white friends, and to denounce them as unworthy of our confidence, looks high and mighty enough on paper; but unless the back ground is filled up with facts demonstrating our independence and self-sustaining power, of what use is such display of self-consequence? Brother DELANY has worked

---

1   *vassalage* Subordination.

2   *their acts* Delany refers to the federal Fugitive Slave Act (1850), and various related state laws, which required Northerners to aid in the capture and re-enslavement of individuals found (or suspected) to have escaped slavery.

3   *is a consummation ... be wished* See Shakespeare's *Hamlet* 3.1.72–73.

long and hard—he has written vigorously, and spoken eloquently to colored people—beseeching them, in the name of liberty, and all the dearest interests of humanity, to unite their energies, and to increase their activities in the work of their own elevation; yet where has his voice been heeded? and where is the practical result? Echo answers, where? Is not the field open? Why, then, should any man object to the efforts of Mrs. Stowe, or anyone else, who is moved to do anything on our behalf? The assertion that Mrs. Stowe "knows nothing about us," shows that Bro. DELANY knows nothing about Mrs. Stowe, for he certainly would not so violate his moral, or common sense if he did. When Brother DELANY will submit any plan for benefitting the colored people, or will candidly criticise any plan already submitted, he will be heard with pleasure. But we expect no plan from him. He has written a book—and we may say that it is, in many respects, an excellent book—on the condition, character, and destiny of the colored people,[1] but it leaves us just where it finds us, without chart or compass, and in more doubt and perplexity than before we read it.

Brother Delany is one of our strong men; and we are therefore all the more grieved, that at a moment when all our energies should be united in giving effect to the benevolent designs of our friends, his voice should be uplifted to strike a jarring note, or to awaken a feeling of distrust.

In respect to a national convention, we are for it—and will not only go "ten miles," but a thousand, if need be, to attend it. Away, therefore, with all unworthy flings on that score.—ED.[2]

PITTSBURGH, April 15th, 1853

...

It is now certain, that the Rev. JOSIAH HENSON, of Dawn, Canada West, is the real *Uncle Tom*, the Christian hero, in Mrs. Stowe's far-famed book of "Uncle Tom's Cabin."[3] Mr. Henson is well

---

1   *a book ... colored people*   Douglass refers to Delany's *The Condition, Elevation, Emigration, and Destiny of the Colored People of the United States, Politically Considered* (1852).
2   *ED.*   Presumably "Editor"; i.e., Douglass.
3   *Rev. JOSIAH HENSON ... Uncle Tom's Cabin*   Josiah Henson (1789–1883) escaped slavery and fled to Canada in 1830, becoming a prominent black leader and abolitionist. His autobiography *The Life of Josiah Henson* (1849) was widely believed to have inspired Stowe's

known to both you and I, and what is said of him in Mrs. S.'s "Key," as far as we are acquainted with the man, and even the opinion we might form of him from our knowledge of his character, we know, or at least believe, to be true to the letter.

Now, what I simply wish to suggest to you, is this: Since Mrs. Stowe and Messrs. Jewett & Co.,[1] Publishers have realized so great an amount of money from the sale of a work founded upon this good old man, whose *living testimony* has to be brought to sustain this great book—and believing that the publishers have realized *five dollars* to the authoress' *one*—would it be expecting too much to suggest, that they—the *publishers*—present Father Henson—for by that name we all know him—with at least *five thous*—now, I won't name any particular sum—but a portion of the profits? I do not know what you may think about it; but it strikes me that this would be but just and right.

I have always thought that George and Eliza were Mr. Henry Bibb and his first wife, with the character of Mr. Lewis Hayden, his wife Harriet and little son, who also effected their escape from Kentucky, under the auspices of Delia Webster, and that martyr philanthropist, Calvin Fairbanks, now incarcerated in a Kentucky State's prison dungeon.[2] I say the *person* of Bibb with the *character* of Hayden; because, in personal appearance of stature and color, as well as circumstances, Bibb answers precisely to George; while he stood quietly by, as he tells us in his own great narrative[3]—and it is a *great book*—with a hoe in his hand, begging his master to desist, while he *stripped his wife's clothes off (!!!)* and lacerated her flesh, until the blood flowed in pools at her feet! To the contrary, had this been Hayden—who, by the way, is not like Bibb nearly *white*, but *black*—he would have buried the hoe deep in the master's skull, laying him lifeless at his feet.

---

novel—a rumor which Stowe herself confirmed in 1853 in her *A Key to Uncle Tom's Cabin*, in which she defended the factual basis for her depictions of Southern slavery.

1   *Messrs. Jewett & Co.*   Boston-based publishers of *Uncle Tom's Cabin*.

2   *Mr. Henry Bibb ... prison dungeon*   Abolitionist Henry Bibb (1815–54) was born into slavery in Kentucky and fled to Canada; Lewis (1811–89) and Harriet Hayden (1816–93) also escaped slavery in Kentucky, aided by Underground Railroad operators Delia Webster (1817–1904) and Calvin Fairbank (1816–98). Webster and Fairbank both faced imprisonment for their activities, Webster for only two months, and Fairbank for a total of nineteen years over various periods.

3   *his own great narrative*   Bibb's *Narrative of the Life and Adventures of Henry Bibb* (1849).

I am of the opinion that Mrs. Stowe has draughted[1] largely on all of the best fugitive slave narratives—at least on Douglass's, Brown's, Bibb's, and perhaps Clark's,[2] as well as the living household of old Father Henson; but of this I am not competent to judge, not having as yet *read* "Uncle Tom's Cabin," *my wife* having *told* me the most I know about it. But these draughts on your narratives, clothed in Mrs. Stowe's own language, only make her work the more valuable, as it is the more *truthful.*

The "negro language," attributed to Uncle Tom by the authoress, makes the character more natural for a slave; but I would barely state, that Father Josiah Henson makes use of as good language, as any one in a thousand Americans.

The probability is, that either to make the story the more affecting, or to conceal the facts of the old man's still being alive, Mrs. Stowe closed his earthly career in New Orleans; but a fact which the publishers may not know: *Father Henson is still a slave* by the laws of the United States—a fugitive slave in Canada. It may be but justice to him to say that I have neither seen nor heard directly or indirectly from Father Henson since September, 1851—then, I was in Toronto, Canada.

The person of Father Henson will increase the valuation of Mrs. Stowe's work very much in England, as he is well known, and highly respected there. His son, Josiah Henson, Jr., is still in England, having accompanied his father there in the winter of 1850.

I may perhaps have made freer use of your and the other names herein mentioned, than what was altogether consonant with your feelings; but I didn't ask you—that's all. Yours for God and Humanity,

M.R. DELANY

---

1 *draughted* Drawn upon; taken inspiration from.
2 *Douglass's ... Clark's* I.e., Frederick Douglass's *Narrative of the Life of Frederick Douglass* (1845), William Wells Brown's *Narrative of William W. Brown* (1847), and Lewis G. Clarke's *Narrative of the Sufferings of Lewis Clarke* (1845).

FREDERICK DOUGLASS, ESQ: DEAR SIR: ... In saying in my letter of the 22nd of March, that "Mrs. Stowe knows nothing about us—'the *Free* Colored People of the United States'—neither does any white person," I admit the expression to be ironical, and not intended to be taken in its literal sense; but I meant to be understood in so saying, that they know nothing, comparatively, about us, to the intelligent, reflecting, general observers among the Free Colored People of the North. And while I readily admit that I "know nothing about Mrs. Stowe," I desire very much to *learn* something of her; and as I could not expect it of Mrs. Stowe, to do so, were she in the country at present,[1] I may at least ask it of brother Douglass, and hope that he will neither consider it derogatory to Mrs. Stowe's position nor attainments, to give me the required information concerning her. I go beyond the mere point of asking it as a favor; I demand it as a right—from you I mean—as I am an interested party, and however humble, may put such reasonable questions to the other party—looking upon you, in this case, as the attorney of said party—as may be necessary to the pending proceedings.

First, then, *assertion*; is not Mrs. Stowe a *Colonizationist?*[2] having so avowed, or at least subscribed to, and recommended their principles in her great work of Uncle Tom.

Secondly; although Mrs. Stowe has ably, eloquently and pathetically[3] portrayed some of the sufferings of the slave, is it any evidence that she has any sympathy for his thrice-morally crucified, semi-free brethren anywhere, or of the *African race* at all; when in the same world-renowned and widely circulated work, she sneers at Haiti—the only truly free and independent civilized black nation as such, or

---

1   *were she ... at present* Stowe was at this time undertaking a promotional tour of England and continental Europe.

2   *is not ... Colonizationist* Throughout the early- to mid-1800s, a number of movements—especially that led by the American Colonization Society, which founded Liberia—arose in the United States, encouraging free blacks to leave the country and colonize Africa. Those who supported such movements claimed that free blacks would have better opportunities abroad than in the United States. Stowe portrays emigration to Liberia positively in *Uncle Tom's Cabin*, though her thoughts on the issue changed over the years, and she eventually renounced colonization (partly as a result of her correspondence with Douglass).

3   *pathetically* Evoking pathos; affectingly.

colored if you please, on the face of the earth—at the same time holding up the little dependent colonization settlement of Liberia in high estimation? I must be permitted to draw my own conclusions, when I say that I can see no other cause for this singular discrepancy in Mrs. Stowe's interest in the colored race, than that one is independent of, and the other subservient to, white men's power.[1]

You will certainly not consider this idea *farfetched*, because it is true American policy; and I do not think it strange, even of Mrs. Stowe, for following in a path so conspicuous, as almost to become the principal public highway. At least, no one will dispute its being a *well-trodden path*. ...

Lastly; the Industrial Institution in contemplation by Mrs. Stowe, for the tuition of colored youth, proposed, as I understand it, the entire employment of white instructors. This I strongly object to, as having a tendency to engender in our youth a higher degree of respect and confidence for white persons than for those of their own color; and creates the impression that colored persons are incapable of teaching, and only suited to *subordinate* positions. I have observed carefully, in all of my travels in our country—in all the schools that I visited—colored schools I mean—that in those taught in whole or part by colored persons, the pupils were always the most respectful towards me, and the less menial in their general bearing. I do not object to white teachers in part; but I do say that wherever competent colored teachers could be obtained for any of the departments, they should be employed. Self-respect begets *due* obedience to others; and obedience is the first step to *self-government* among any people. Certainly, this should be an essential part of the training of our people, separated in interests as we have been, in this country. All the rude and abominable ideas that exist among us, in *preferences for color*, have been engendered *from the whites*, and in God's name, I ask them to do nothing more to increase this absurdity.

Another consideration, is, that all of the pecuniary advantages arising from this position go into the pockets of white men and women,

---

1   *one is independent ... white men's power*   Haiti had declared its independence from France following the black-led Haitian Revolution (1791–1804), while Liberia had declared its own independence from the United States in 1847—but the U.S. did not recognize either country's independence until 1862.

thereby depriving colored persons, so far, of this livelihood. This is the same old song sung over again,
  "Dimes and dollars—dollars and dimes."
And I will say, without the fear of offence, that nothing that has as yet been gotten up by our friends, for the assistance of the colored people of the United States, has even been of any pecuniary benefit to them. Our white friends take care of *that* part. There are, to my knowledge, two exceptions to this allegation—Douglass' printing establishment, and the "Alleghany Institute;"[1] the one having a colored man at the head, and in the other, the assistant being a colored man. …

Let me say another thing, brother Douglass; that is, that no enterprize, institution, or anything else, should be commenced *for us*, or our general benefit, without *first consulting us*. By this I mean consulting the various communities of the colored people in the United States, by such a correspondence as should make public the measure, and solicit their general interests and coincidence. In this way, the intelligence and desires of the whole people would be elicited, and an intelligent understanding of their real desires obtained. Other than this, is treating us as slaves, and presupposing us all to be ignorant, and incapable of knowing our own *wants*. Many of the measures of our friends have failed from this very cause; and I am fearful that many more will fail.

In conclusion, brother Douglass, let me say, that I am the last person among us who would wilfully "strike a jarring note, or awaken a feeling of distrust," uncalled for; and although you may pronounce it "unwise, ungraceful, and sounding high and mighty on paper"; as much high respect as an humble simple-minded person should have for them, and as much honored as I should feel in having such names enrolled as our benefactors—associated with our degraded position in society; believe me when I tell you, that I speak it as a son, a brother, a husband and a father; I speak it from the consciousness of oppressed humanity, outraged manhood, of a degraded husband and disabled father; I speak it from the recesses of a wounded bleeding heart—in the name of my wife and children, who look to me for

---

1 *Alleghany Institute* College, later called Avery College after its white founder Charles Avery (1784–1858), offering higher education to African Americans; John Peck (1802–75), a black abolitionist, was among the school's board of trustees.

protection, as the joint partner of our humble fireside; I say, if this great fund and aid are to be sent here to foster and aid the schemes of the American Colonization Society, as I say to you—I say with reverence, and an humbleness of feeling, becoming my position, with a bowed-down head, that the benevolent, great and good, the Duchess of Sutherland, Mr. Gurney, their graces the Earl of Shaftesbury and the Earl of Carlisle; had far better retain their money in the Charity Fund of Stafford House,[1] or any other place, than to send it to the United States for any such unhallowed purposes! No person will be more gratified, nor will more readily join in commendation, than I, of any good measure attempted to be carried out by Mrs. Stowe, if the contrary of her colonization principles be disproved. I will not accept *chains* from a king, any sooner than from a peasant; and never shall, willingly, submit to any measures for my own degradation. I am in hopes, brother Douglass, as every one else will understand my true position.

Yours for God and down-trodden Humanity,

M.R. DELANY

[6 May 1853]

The Letter of M. R. Delany [Published on the page preceding Delany's final letter.]

This letter is premature, unfair, uncalled for, and, withal, needlessly long; but, happily it needs not a long reply.

Can brother Delany be the writer of it?—It lacks his generous spirit. The letter is premature, because it attacks a plan, the details of which are yet undefined. It is unfair, because it imputes designs (and replies to them) which have never been declared. It is uncalled for,

---

1   *Duchess of Sutherland ... Stafford House*   The London home of Harriet Elizabeth Georgiana Leveson-Gower (1806–68) was the meeting place of many English abolitionists and other social activists, including Quaker philanthropist Joseph John Gurney (1788–1847), Anthony Ashley-Cooper, Earl of Shaftesbury (1801–85), and George Howard, Earl of Carlisle (1802–64).

because there is nothing in the position of Mrs. Stowe which should awaken against her a single suspicion of unfriendliness towards the free colored people of the United States; but, on the contrary, there is much in it to inspire confidence in her friendship.

The information for which brother Delany asks concerning Mrs. Stowe, he has given himself. He says *she* is a colonizationist; and we ask, what if she is?—names do not frighten us. A little while ago, brother Delany was a colonizationist. If we do not misremember, in his book[1] he declared in favor of colonizing the eastern coast of Africa. Yet, we never suspected his friendliness to the colored people; nor should we feel called upon to oppose any plan he might submit, for the benefit of the colored people, on that account. We recognize friends wherever we find them.

Whoever will bring a straw's weight of influence to break the chains of our brother bondmen, or whisper one word of encouragement and sympathy to our proscribed race in the North, shall be welcomed by us to that philanthropic field of labor. We shall not, therefore, allow the sentiments put in the brief letter of GEORGE HARRIS, at the close of *Uncle Tom's Cabin*,[2] to vitiate forever Mrs. Stowe's power to do us good. Who doubts that Mrs. Stowe is more of an abolitionist now than when she wrote that chapter?—We believe that lady to be but at the beginning of her labors for the colored people of this country.

Brother Delany says, nothing should be done for us, or commenced for us, without "consulting us." Where will he find "*us*" to consult with? Through what organization, or what channel could such consulting be carried on? Does he mean by consulting "*us*" that nothing is to be done for the improvement of the colored people in general, without consulting each colored man in the country whether it shall be done? *How many*, in this case, constitute "*us*"? Evidently brother Delany is a little unreasonable here.

Four years ago, a proposition was made, through the columns of *The North Star*,[3] for the formation of a "*National League*," and a

---

1   *his book* I.e., *The Condition, Elevation, Emigration, and Destiny of the Colored People of the United States, Politically Considered* (1852).

2   *brief letter … Uncle Tom's Cabin* At the end of the novel, the formerly enslaved George Harris emigrates to Liberia, and sends back a letter explaining and justifying his decision.

3   *The North Star* Douglass's previous newspaper, which evolved into *Frederick Douglass' Paper* in 1851.

constitution for said League was drawn up, fully setting forth a plan for united, intelligent and effective co-operation on the part of the free colored people of the United States—a body capable of being "*consulted.*" The colored people, in their wisdom, or in their indifference, gave the scheme little or no encouragement—and it failed. Now, we happen to know that such an organization as was then proposed, was enquired for, and sought for by Mrs. Harriet Beecher Stowe; she wished, most of all, to hear from such a body *what could* be done for the *free colored people* of the United States? But there was no such body to answer.

The fact is, brother Delany, we are a disunited and scattered people, and very much of the responsibility of this disunion must fall upon such colored men as yourself and the writer of this. We want more confidence in each other, as a race—more self-forgetfulness, and less disposition to find fault with well-meant efforts for our benefit. Mr. Delany knows that, at this moment, he could call a respectable Convention of the free colored people of the Northern States. Why don't he issue his call? and he knows, too, that, were we to issue such a call, it would instantly be regarded as an effort to promote the interests of our *paper.* This consideration, and a willingness on our part to occupy an obscure position in such a movement, has led us to refrain from issuing a call. *The Voice of the Fugitive*, we observe, has suggested the holding, in New York, of a "World's Convention" during the "World's Fair."[1] A better proposition, we think, would be to hold in that city a "National Convention" of the colored people. Will not friend Delany draw up a call for such a Convention, and send it to us for publication?

But to return. Brother Delany asks, if we should allow "*anybody*" to undertake measures for our elevation? YES, we answer—anybody, even a slaveholder. Why not? Then says brother Delany, why not accept the measures of "Gurley and Pinney"?[2] We answer, simply because *their measures* do not commend themselves to our judgment.

---

1   *The Voice of the Fugitive* Antislavery newspaper founded by Henry Bibb in Canada in 1851; *World's Fair* The Exhibition of the Industry of All Nations was held in New York in 1853.

2   *Gurley and Pinney* Ralph Randolph Gurley (1797–1872) and John Brooke Pinney (1806–82), ministers in the Presbyterian Church and prominent members of the American Colonization Society.

That is all. If "Gurley and Pinney" would establish an industrial college, where colored young men could learn useful trades, with a view to their becoming useful men and respectable citizens of the United States, we should applaud them and co-operate with them.

We don't object to Colonizations because they express a lively interest in the civilization and Christianization of Africa; nor because they desire the prosperity of Liberia; but it is because, like brother Delany, they have not sufficient faith in the people of the United States to believe that the black man can ever get justice at their hands on American soil. It is because they have systematically, and almost universally, sought to spread their hopelessness among the free colored people themselves; and thereby rendered them, if not contented with, at least resigned to the degradation which they have been taught to believe must be perpetual and immutable, while they remain where they are. It is because, having denied the possibility of our elevation here, they have sought to make good this denial, by encouraging the enactment of laws subjecting us to the most flagrant outrages, and stripping us of all the safeguards necessary to the security of our liberty, persons and property. We say all this of the American Colonization Society; but we are *far* from saying this of many who speak and wish well to Liberia. As to the imputation that all the pecuniary profit arising out of the industrial scheme will probably pass into the pockets of the whites, it will be quite time enough to denounce such a purpose when such a purpose is avowed. But we have already dwelt too long on a letter which perhaps carried its own answer with it.

From the Publisher

A name never says it all, but the word "Broadview" expresses a good deal of the philosophy behind our company. We are open to a broad range of academic approaches and political viewpoints. We pay attention to the broad impact book publishing and book printing has in the wider world; for some years now we have used 100% recycled paper for most titles. Our publishing program is internationally oriented and broad-ranging. Our individual titles often appeal to a broad readership too; many are of interest as much to general readers as to academics and students.

Founded in 1985, Broadview remains a fully independent company owned by its shareholders—not an imprint or subsidiary of a larger multinational.

To order our books or obtain up-to-date information, please visit broadviewpress.com.

broadview press
www.broadviewpress.com

This book is made of paper from well-managed FSC® - certified forests, recycled materials, and other controlled sources.